Mama Ain't Always Right!

A JOURNEY TO FORGIVENESS

Unforgiveness is an illness. Forgiveness is the Cure

Evangelist Brenda Henderson

Copyright©2021 By Evangelist Brenda Henderson

Mama Ain't Always Right! A Journey to Forgiveness

Printed in the United States of America ISBN 978-1-7357018-1-3

All rights reserved solely by the author. The author guarantees all contents are original and do not infringe upon legal rights of any other person or work. No part of this book may be reproduced in any form without the permission of the author.

Unless otherwise indicated, Scripture quotations are taken from The Holy Bible's King Jams Version (KJV). Copyright ©2011 Biblical, Inc. Used by permission. All rights reserved.

This is a work of fiction. Names, characters, businesses, places, events and incidents are either the products of the author's imagination or used in a fictitious manner. Any resemblance to actual persons, living or dead, or actual events is purely coincidental.

Editor: Edits By Bakeba

www.editsbybakeba.com

Rich Book Business Publishing & Coaching

www.richrelationshipsus.com

TABLE OF CONTENTS

ACKNOWLEDGMENTS 1

PREFACE..2

THE INNER FLOW..5

CHAPTER ONE: UNFORGIVENESS 7

CHAPTER TWO: IN THE BEGINNING 20

CHAPTER THREE: IN THE MIDDLE 37

CHAPTER FOUR: HOW HIGH, HOW LOW 59

CHAPTER FIVE: IT'S MY THING, DO WHAT I WANNA DO
....91

CHAPTER SIX: THE FIRST TWO YEARS 121

CHAPTER SEVEN: TWO MORE YEARS 132

CHAPTER EIGHT: IN A FEW MORE YEARS................153

CHAPTER NINE: AFTER THE BALL.................................171

CHAPTER TEN: THE NEXT CHAPTER 196

CHAPTER ELEVEN: ALL THAT GLITTERS AIN'T GOAL 232

CHAPTER TWELVE: ONWARD...265

ACKNOWLEDGMENTS

Much love to all my readers who have supported me in my previous literary works, Preying Men: The Art of Christian Deception; Preying Men 2: Facing Cain; and My Worth Book and to my family, my NJC church family and friends.

Special thanks to Renée Beavers and her Superhero, Gil, who have under-girded me on this project.

It is my prayer that as you read this book, you too will take the Journey to Forgiveness.

For if ye forgive men their trespasses, your heavenly Father will also forgive you: But if ye forgive NOT men their trespasses, neither will your Father forgive your trespasses Matthew 6:14-15.

PREFACE

Let me start with the word, UNFORGIVENESS. Unforgiveness is when you are unwilling or unable to forgive someone for hurting, betraying, breaking your trust or causing you intense pain. Some of us are far into our adulthood before we become such cynics on the subject matter that awaits you in this book.

Unfortunately, my cynicism began early on as a child. It was imposed upon me by my adoptive mother and to seal the deal, she laced it with fear. Fear embedded in you as a child is still there when you grow up. It's already enough to have world problems, relationship problems and parenting problems but to handle them in fear can lead to bad decisions— decisions that will cause you to continue to "just go with the flow" of things to avoid conflict, all while feeling trapped and in bondage. The more trapped you become, the more unforgiveness you store away. It is stored in your emotional memory, in the marks that have been physically left on your body. It is powerful and it can overtake you.

Many who carry the illness of unforgiveness have refused to seek help. Instead, they have chosen to live with the pain and anguish of hurting behind the hurt. I have learned that hurting people always hurt others. Although we are not always intending to reenact the unforgiveness hurt, more often than we would like to admit, we do. I did.

My reaction to unforgiveness has always been feeling minimal self-worth. I was raised to think that I was not worth much unless I was told by my mother what I was exactly worth. Through the process, the journey to forgiveness, I needed the Lord to guide me so I would survive. It began when I engulfed the explanation of Psalms 139:14: *I will praise thee; for I am fearfully and wonderfully made: marvelous are they works; and that my soul knoweth right well.* I inhaled this scripture until I finally injected it into my system. I was worthy, and more importantly, I was worthy to God. I suppose I thought that was all I needed to do--was find my worth to forgive. Correcting a problem with one method, does not guarantee that other assistance might still be needed. And it was. What was needed for me were three things:

Confession-Admitting I hadn't totally forgiven her; Expression-Talking about how I felt; and Testimony- Sharing with others, who have unforgiveness in their hearts, how God brought me over.

The story is fictitious by nature, yet factual by relatability. You will follow the life of Bea Coral Faye who has been deceived by her mother and spent most of her life trying to live according to her rules. It takes a while but she learns how to abide under the shadow of the Almighty. Better yet, she learns how to cure her illness of unforgiveness.

First and foremost, I would like to thank my Heavenly Father who told me to write stories. I told Him He had the wrong person. He keeps showing me that He does not. All to Him, I owe.

THE INNER FLOW

You probably don't know me but some of you will identify with me. Actually, I know I've already identified with some of you. I'm Bea Coral Faye and I keep showing up in books designed to help you--that reflect you and then, set you free. My first appearance was in Preying Men: The Art of Christian Deception. I married a man who professed to be a man of God. He fit the profile but led a deceptive lifestyle. This godly man had wicked hands laced with drugs, murder, rape and another wife. The next time I showed up was in Preying Men 2: Facing Cain. By all practical purposes, this joker, Cain Mitchel, was supposed to be dead. Instead, he returned unrecognizable to try and destroy me and others who were close to me. But God! Oh, God completely delivered me from Cain but He didn't deliver me from me.

You see, I had to put in some real work for my deliverance. I had to focus on the reason why I didn't see any of this chaos coming. But let me tell you something. When the chaos came and went, I stood laying blame. I blamed my upbringing by an emotionally, physically and verbally abusive mother for my misfortunes. She was the blame for me being so connected to fear, for my insecurity, unworthiness and even for my hopelessness. Yeah, I laid blame for many years until the Lord pointed out to me (when I thought I did the work and forgave her) that I was merely punching the clock. I had to go back, all the way back and learn how to forgive.

I have been blessed with a beautiful family. A Godly husband that is the real deal and a bright, handsome and anointed son. All seemed perfect with my life until my unfinished un-forgiveness forced me to take that long journey to COMPLETE forgiveness. Won't you come and take the journey with me? You might discover that you've just been punching the clock, too. There is still hope and there is still time for you to forgive.

Chapter One
UNFORGIVENESS

My name is Bea Coral Faye Parker. My husband is Earl Parker, Jr. and we have one son whose name is David.

David is ten years old now and has great spiritual insight. For instance, he knows when Earl and I are not standing in total agreement about something and he will look at both of us and say, "Mom? Dad? Did you guys pray together so that you can come to an agreement about whatever it is you're disagreeing about?" Somehow God has chosen to give us a son after His own heart. He is bright and full of life as well as the love of God. We are so blessed as parents.

We formally lived in a small town called Cashew in the State of Texas and we were faithful members of Temple of Praise where the Bishop D. J. Paul was the Presiding Bishop. As a matter of fact, Earl worked for the entire District as the supervisor over maintenance for the District's Member Churches. I worked as the Public Relations (PR) Director for Temple of Praise (TOP).

An incredible amount of unholy circumstances occurred while in Cashew. When I tell you that place was loaded with drama, it is not just my imagination. According to the town's gossip, I was framed, hunted, found, died and came back to life all in Cashew. Additionally, the residue of my prior marriage to Cain Mitchell ran havoc over our lives. Earl had long since been weary of the place and was more than ready to move away. We sold our home while the market was good and moved to a smaller town--Augusta, Texas.

Augusta was farther north of Cashew and its population was barely one hundred thousand residents. It is so peaceful and quiet. The school system here is one of the best in the State and we are strong advocates for education, so for us, this was a plus. Now, that all the location information has been given and the gratefulness to God has been expressed, on with the business of exposing my childhood and putting together pieces that haunt me and cause me to act out of character sometimes. I can be as gentle as a lamb and then suddenly, I become a roaring lioness for no reason. Poor Earl has the patience of Job and puts up with my split personality episodes as if they don't bother him but I know they do. Lately, I have been lashing out at my son, David, over simple things that are not major issues; yet, I find a way to turn it into one.

It is a fact that I am a praying woman and I have gone to God with all of this and for a while, I could not find an answer. Then early one morning, just before the break of dawn, I heard Him say, "You must forgive and you have not."

Puzzled, I asked, "Forgive who? Forgive what?" (If you've ever had a conversation with God, you know that He only talks so much and then, the rest is left to your faith and trust in Him.) I pondered over this forgiveness thing for weeks.

Am I Good Enough

Right off the bat, I had no idea who I hadn't forgiven until David had an unpleasant experience at school. On that day, the students in his class were presenting posters that outlined their aspirations and goals for the future. David has always expressed (after watching millions of old episodes of Perry Mason and Ironside with his father) that he wanted to become a lawyer, but even beyond that, a Supreme Court Justice. Earl and I had helped him construct a visual that highlighted Thurgood Marshall, along with Johnny Cochran, and even a photo of David in a judge's robe. His teacher thought it was brilliant and quite informative.

One student in the class blurted out after the presentation, "You've got to be kidding me David Parker! You are too dark to be a Supreme Court Justice!"

Trying not to breakdown, David responded by saying, "But Justice Thurgood Marshall was an African American Judge! Didn't you know that?"

The boy yelled again, "I'm not talking about race. I am talking about skin color. Somebody as dark as you will never sit on that bench." "My Dad says that the only reason Marshall was on there was because he was light skinned."

"Alright then, what about Clarence Thomas? His skin is dark."

"Yea, but that's okay because he's a Republican!" The classroom roared with laughter.

David was so hurt and defeated. His teacher had the principal come in and remove the boy from the classroom and called his parents. But by that time, the damage had already been done.

"Mom, do you think I'm too dark to become a Supreme Court Justice?"

"Of course not, where is that question coming from?" David took his time and relived the whole incident for me. I was furious but for the sake of behaving like a civilized mom instead of a psycho one, I tried to comfort him with these words, "Regardless of skin color, with a good education, you can become whoever you choose to be."

"Are you sure, Mom?"

"Yes, I am sure." He smiled and hurried to his room to finish homework before dinner.

When Earl came home, I told him about David's experience and all he said was, "God is teaching David that everyone is not going to like him because he is chosen and set apart. He's not like everyone else. He must learn to believe in himself from here on out. He cannot afford to let what others say block his blessings. He is only ten years old and he has a long way to go. With God's guidance, he will become what is predestined for him to become. I will talk to him about it later this evening. But right now, I need to give my beautiful wife a kiss, take a shower and get ready for a good home cooked meal."

"Umm, what smells so good?" Earl tried to kiss me. I pushed him away.

"Is that all you can say is that God is teaching him that he is not like everyone else? Our son was humiliated today in front of his peers by the use of racial identification and undertones and this is your only explanation!!? How dare you blow this off!"

"I am not blowing it off, Bea. I said I would talk to him about it. I'm sure the other kid was reprimanded and is suspended for such behavior, after all the administration is intolerant of these types of behaviors at his school. I apologize if I don't seem so filled with anger like you are but the incident is over and I will make sure it doesn't happen again. I swear I don't know what triggers these outbursts but I am praying that there's a method to this madness that you are experiencing."

Earl went upstairs to get ready for dinner. Then, it hit me: The unforgiveness I had in my heart was for my Mother. She would tell me that I would never amount to anything. I wanted a career in Public Relations but she thought that was a stupid idea. Her plans were that I become a schoolteacher because they made a lot of money. She had no idea that teachers were the lowest paid on the totem pole. My Mother had the mindset that she was always right and there was no convincing her otherwise. What was worse was the physical abuse that she used to persuade me just in case I thought she was wrong. As she lay dying, many years later, I told her, "I forgive you Mama, I forgive you." Perhaps I thought I forgave her but in my heart of hearts, I did not.

I Refuse to Recreate the Misery

I am growing older and there is one thing I don't want to do and that's to die with unforgiveness in my heart. It would not be beneficial to my husband nor my son to allow the brokenness of unforgiveness recreate the miserable life I lived early on. I had no idea what love really looked like in the Spirit until I finally understood the unconditional love that God has for me. It's hard to say when I transitioned from understanding it to believing it. I tried all my life to please my Mother. I longed for praise or warm hugs from her. Inside, I often questioned how was God going to love me if my own Mother didn't love me? I suppose there is a margin of possibility that she really did love me. But it was in an obsessive, verbally, and physically abusive way. But one can count that as love, though, right? If love cusses you, smothers you, restricts you, belittles you, criticizes you and then tries to knock the breath out of you, is it still love? Or was it my Mother's love/hate reaction to her own deep embedded hurt? Was it the pain and suffering that she experienced as a child and now that she has a child of her own, this was the only way she knew how to raise her?

Whatever the case may be, I lived a life filled with fear until I was almost thirty years old. Everything in my life was affected and infected by my Mother. Experiencing everything from cussings, whippings that left visual marks, even exposing my flesh, to preventing possible friendships that I could have made. Even my very first attempt at marriage was sabotaged by my Mother. Perhaps this was the only way she knew how to love me but this was not the way I wanted to show David and Earl how I loved them. These emotional flare ups must stop! I know the Lord for myself and I know He can help me love myself through this.

The most amazing thing my Mother did exactly right was introduce me to the Lord. Although, her actions were a contradiction to her "church appearances", she did a really good job teaching me who He was and how important it was to always keep Him at the center of my life. I loved to read so the Bible was a welcomed challenge for me to tackle. When I saw the miracles, sights and wonders in that Book, I began to daydream about a beautiful place called Heaven and how, by any means necessary, I had to get there. I am still on that journey, as well as, the journey to completely forgive my Mother. It's amazing how one can think you have completed a task; yet, some of it has been left undone.

The fear of my Mother has been the blame for my insecurities, my poor choices in men, my avoidance of taking risks and my ability to hurt people with my words. I even blame her for my claustrophobia. (If I complained while she was washing my hair, she'd hold my head under water until I stopped. I never learned how to swim, even until this day, because of this.)

I don't believe that this is who God made me to be. I believe God is trying to grow me into understanding that all I encountered in my past was necessary and that total forgiveness is in order for my present and my future. It is my goal to reach way deep down inside of me, forgive my Mother and appreciate the strength her behavior gave me. It is apparent that I can no longer use how she raised me as an excuse for my shortcomings but what I can do is share my experiences of my childhood into adulthood life as a testimony of just what God's power can do!

So Grateful for My Life

Here I am, fully grown with a wonderful God-fearing husband and an amazing son. I live a favored and blessed life. I no longer work on a full-time basis and Earl provides above and beyond for all of us. As a matter of fact, when we relocated, the District had already employed Earl as the Executive Director of Church Services for the entire Northern District Region. The salary package is well over six figures and the cost of living here, in Augusta, is much lower than it was in Cashew. I work part-time as an at-home PR Assistant for TOP because I enjoy public relations work and I don't mind helping them out in a pinch. Besides, it's all done electronically and I never have to leave the house. Yet, every time I think about how my Mother tried to impress upon me failure, I thank God that I kept pushing and fighting my way through. I finished college with both a Bachelor's and Master's in Business and never considered being a teacher of any type, well…maybe once. (But we will talk about this later.)

In my hometown of Seawall, TX, I worked at a small PR business which did quite well. Even after relocating to Cashew, God had a good job waiting for me and I was hired before I moved there. Not bad for a little girl who wasn't going to succeed in this world unless she took her Mother's advice and became a schoolteacher. In my maturing, I now feel sad for my Mom and have since come to realize that she was just miserable.

I am not sure what happened in her childhood that made her so angry (although now as an adult, I've developed my own theory) all the time but whatever it was, she made sure she relived the anger through me. She said I was going to be stupid and man-crazy like my biological mother whom she said, "Could not be without a man."

The Beginning

Oh, I'm sorry, I'm getting ahead of myself. The Mother of whom I speak was my adoptive mother, my great aunt. When she decided to share the adoption story with me, I was around age seven. The scenario she painted about why she had to adopt me made it sound as if I was knocking at death's door. I was one child too many for my biological Mom because she was too preoccupied with men to take care of her youngest baby girl. My (adoptive) Mother only had a fourth- grade education and so she bullied her way through life. Just like she probably bullied my Mother out of giving me to her. However, I finally connected with my birth family although, I never laid eyes on my biological Mom until my adoptive mother started experiencing stages of dementia. Also, one night my oldest sister contacted me by phone.

People often talk about good intentions. I am sure my Mother had intentions, whether they were all good or not, is questionable. There were unbelievable restrictions on my life and reoccurring feelings of guilt concerning how she "saved" me from a horrible life and unbearable situations. She instilled in me that I owed her for everything she had ever done for me and I spent most of my life trying to pay her back.

At an early age, I was quite animated and I read well. Our church had a District Congress every year and there were several categories you could enter according to your age group. For my age group, it was Bible Storytelling and Bible Memory Work. A nice lady by the name of Sis. Niece was over the Youth Department and she chose whom she felt was gifted for each category. She also gave us the material we needed to study and practice. On Sunday evenings at Bible Training Union (BTU), she made sure that we rehearsed so that we memorized our Bible verses and, in my case, the Bible story. Back then, I had what you called a photographic memory so once I received my story, I would take photos of it in my head and knew it word for word in record time. (Oh, to be young again.)

Mama, Why Don't You Care?

It was the day of the Congress and it was finally my turn. Like I said, I was animated so I not only told the story but I performed it while reciting it. My first story was Noah and the Ark. I can't remember whether I made animal noises or faces but I do remember that I won First Place. I just knew Mama would be so proud. Sis. Niece told Mama that I had won First Place and that she should have been there to hear me. Her only reply was, "Why did I need to be there to hear her? I heard her say it every damn day!"

My little heart sank inside my body. I wanted to cry but I knew if I cried, it would only make her angry and I didn't like her when she was angry. Sis. Niece felt sorry for me. I could tell by the way she looked. There I stood, a little girl wanting her mother to be proud of her when she could have cared less. Sis. Niece went on to tell her how proud the entire church was of me and that the First-Place ribbon proved that I was the best in the Bible Storytelling Category.

"I hope you don't mind if I start preparing Bea for next year's competition. By far, she is amazing and Pastor could not be prouder. All the kids did extremely well but it was just something about Bea that stood out."

My Mom lit a cigarette, blew out a puff of smoke and said, "Thanks for taking her. I'll let you know about next year." She walked away and left Sis. Niece and me just standing there.

"Alright, well thank you for letting her go", her voice straining trying to make sure Mama heard her.

She looked at me and said, "You did real good Bea. Everyone is so proud of you. I'll be on my way now." She gave me a big hug and went out the front door as if to say, 'That poor child, why doesn't her Mother acknowledge the good things that she does?'

If she could have answered that question for me right then and there, there would be no need for forgiveness. But she couldn't answer it for me nor could I answer it for myself. I often thought that my Mother didn't really want me. Yet, she chose to adopt me from her very own niece. I tried to be happy and filled with joy but it was so difficult when I was confined to a household with such brokenness and bitterness: she was so bitter that even the bitterness in her could not be broken. It seemed as if there was no pleasing her, no making her happy, never making her proud. It's as if that's what she programmed me to do and if I did please her, make her happy or make her proud, I would be punished.

Kind words spoken from her lips were few and far between. I think she thought that if she praised me or said something nice to me, I would take advantage of her in some way. Take advantage of her…that would be an enormous mistake! I was terrified of her! She stood almost six feet tall even and she was strong. My two hands could fit inside one of her hands. She cussed like a sailor and swung like a New York Yankee. She could hit you with a closed fist and give you a concussion. She could slap you with the back of her hand and swell your face up. There was no way I would intentionally cross my

Mother. To cross her simply meant that I was ready to commit suicide. I felt there were some horrible things that happened to me at the hands of my Mother but there were some good things, too. She made sure that every gift she thought I had was developed through activities at church, whether she attended them or not.

I was accustomed to going to church all day on Sundays. Sunday School, Morning Worship, sometimes a three o'clock service when the church was invited out, BTU at six and then Evening worship beginning at seven. Traditional Baptist folks, back in the day, would disagree with the extended church services of the Pentecostals. Yet, when it came to that staying all day and night stuff, Baptist were next of kin to the Pentecostals! Oh yeah, don't let me be reminded of all the mid-week activities Baptist had going on. The Baptist were neck-in-neck with our Christian counterparts. There was Mission ministries on Monday, Usher meetings on Tuesday, teachers' meeting on Wednesday, choir rehearsal on Thursday and children's choir rehearsal on Saturday. So to me, Baptist folks complaining about the long extensive services of the Pentecostals' extended services is like the pot trying to call the kettle black! I admit that they sang and danced and played loud instruments but it sure sounded like they were having a lot more fun than we were. In life, I learned there is more than one way to praise the Lord.

Chapter Two

IN THE BEGINNING

I heard Madelene's, my adoptive Mom, version of how and why my adoption took place and thirty years later I heard the true version.

So, for timeline's sake, I would like to begin with the version Madelene gave me. (I promise, you'll hear the true version later.) She painted a picture of doom and gloom that engulfed my thoughts so heavily until I believed if she hadn't rescued me, I would have died. She told me that my malnourishment wouldn't allow me to stand up properly, even though I was over one and a half years old. "They never kept you clean. Your diaper was filled with pee that ran down your legs which left your ankles black with mildew, dirt, and mold." I was seven years old when she started to tell me of my horrid past: stories about my trifling mother who would open her legs to any man that came along and my four brothers and two sisters who were glad that there was one less mouth to feed.

The first five years after Madelene's rescue, I hadn't spoken a word. This concern prompted her to take me to the doctor because she thought I might be mentally challenged. The doctor assured her there was nothing wrong with me, at all, and that when I chose to talk, I would. And so, it was. One day, my Papa was coming home—walking from the bus stop that was just on the other side of the park in front of our house. When I saw him through the screen door, I screamed, "Papa, Papa!" Mama began to weep and cry out, "Thank you, God! Oh, Thank You JESUS, my baby is alright!"

Of course, I was alright. Although, I can't remember this episode for myself, I assume I didn't want to talk because I had nothing to say. I was probably traumatized from being taken from the only family I'd known since birth. I didn't know who Madelene was, at all. After a while, when it became apparent that there was no other mother nor sisters and brothers, I probably didn't know what to say. Although small, I can remember feeling sad that my real mother, Fannie, didn't want me and had treated me so badly. Not keeping me clean, not feeding me, that felt so hurtful.

I learned quickly that I needed to be grateful for what Madelene had done for me. After all she had saved my life, right? The adoption story allowed Madelene to establish her control over me. She would constantly remind me that "if it hadn't been for her, there would be no me." Through obligation, I tried to do everything she asked; yet, shuddered in fear if she felt I had done it wrong.

My Papa

My Papa, on the other hand, was quite the opposite. His name was Sanford Faye. They called him "Sweets" because he was such a sweet person. He had the most beautiful smile and the kindest heart. Madelene did not want me to have any friends nor go anywhere out of her reach because I should only believe the words that came out of her mouth. EVERYONE else was a liar, including my Papa. Papa came from a large family who believed in having fun. Madelene called it "partying". Therefore, she saw to it that I would never become close to Papa's side of the family.

One glorious day, Papa managed to sneak me over to my cousins' house so I could meet them and know who they were. Madelene would have killed him if she knew that's where we went. He told her that he was taking me to a company picnic given for the employees at his job and he would bring me back before the evening was over. I had so much fun that day. Playing with my cousins—laughing and talking. I felt free. I felt happy. Feeling happy was strange to me so when I experienced a bit of it, I almost lost my mind. Being Madelene's child, I had to find a way to conceal my "so happy" from her once we arrived back home. That was so Papa wouldn't get in trouble for letting me experience so much joy. Therefore, I pretended not to be feeling well and was so tired that I just wanted to take a bath and lie down.

"That's what you get—hanging outdoors with strangers, ain't no telling what they may have given you to eat or drink—the reason you don't feel good."

"Maddy, (that's what Papa called Mama), now you know I was not going to let Bea eat or drink anything that I didn't eat or drink myself. It was a little hot outside and she attempted to try and play with some of the kids but she just doesn't know how to pace herself. She seems so over excited when it comes to playing with other kids and having fun."

"Fun isn't all it's cracked up to be. Especially around other people that don't mean you no good, no how."

Then she told me, "Ain't nobody gone ever love you besides me. You are my little flat nosed baby and you better get that through your head right now."

I spoke just above a whisper and said, "Yes, ma'am."

While she was facing me, I could see Papa wink behind her back at me to let me know he would probably sneak me off again. She never gave him another chance.

"Gone and wash them dishes up and sweep and mop that kitchen floor before you take a bath."

"Maddy, the child is not feeling well. Let her take a bath and go to bed."

"Sanford, if you don't stay out of my business with Bea, I am going to throw you and your things out of this house."

"You act like you the only one who adopted the girl Maddy! My name is on that birth certificate, too! Bea is my daughter just as much as she is yours!"

"The hell she is! Your name may be on her birth certificate but your ass is somewhere in the streets when she's sick or hungry. You better get out of my face!"

It was time for me to exit for real. I was often the subject of their arguments because Papa always tried to defend me. Even as a man, he could not win against Madelene. He would tire before she would and slam the door as he disappeared into the night not returning until morning. It felt like a long time before morning came. I would feel so helpless on those nights when he would disappear for fear that she would whip me, scold me or cuss me out because of something he said to defend me during their arguments. Fortunately, tonight I was not a target because the next day just happened to be Sunday.

Sundays

Whenever Sunday came, Mama would be a lot nicer. She never let me forget the importance of going to church and praying to the Lord. She sang in the choir and participated in the Women's Senior Mission Ministry at the Seawall First Baptist Church. The Rev. Alex Wright was the pastor and people worshipped him. Whatever Rev. Wright said, was right! He could do no wrong. His interpretation of the Bible was their interpretation of the Bible.

As I begin to grow up and understand the Word of God, it was revealed to me that it wasn't so much about what Rev. Wright said but it was about what God said. I became thirsty and hungry for the Word of God and what it could mean to me. Although I had read most of the Bible before, I was just beginning to understand it. I wasn't sure what to call it back then but something or someone was opening my understanding. I begin to zoom in on what the preacher was saying and underlining it in my used Bible from the Goodwill Store that Mama had bought me when we went school shopping one year. When I was done with my homework and my chores, I would read. Yes, Sundays were always a great day for me. By the time we went to Sunday School, Morning Worship, three pm service and back to Night Service, Mama was pooped. On Sunday nights, I was trained to make my lunch, take my bath and lay out my clothes for Monday. Then, I would sleep. Ah, as the late Gospel Singer, Daryl Coley would say, "Whenever Sunday Comes", my mama was a maid, which they now call a domestic worker.

Madelene's Story

Story was that she had been one (a maid) since she was eleven years old—that's when her mother died. I was told by Papa that a white family had taken Mama in and she cleaned and cooked for them. Where were the child labor laws back then? It wasn't until I became an adult that it dawned on me that Mama was probably molested by a male in that family and that may be the reason why she was so mean to Papa. I do remember he told me that my Grandma Cadie, Madelene's mother, told him to marry Madelene and take care of her because she would either kill someone or be killed. He did what Grandma Cadie asked. They were married and moved out of the little country town of Levy to Seawall.

Mama was 14 and Papa was 16. They bought a small lot and built our little house by hand. It had a living room, dining room, kitchen, two bedrooms and a bathroom. It was nothing fancy but it was home. It sat right in front of a park where the neighborhood kids would go and play. They would swing on the swings and ride on the merry-go-round until almost dusk on the weekends.

My Early Years

I sat on the front porch and watched. Every blue moon she would let me go to the park and play with the next door neighbor's child, Lainey. She and I grew up as neighbors and we remain friends to this day. Lainey's mom was so sweet and soft spoken. I never heard her say an unkind word to anyone. Madelene liked Lainey's mom, Mrs. James, so she let us play together sometimes. Those were the days that I felt like an unrestricted child. We would play softball and hide and seek and run races. Of course, I only participated in one or two activities before I would hear my name called followed by a whistle Madelene would blow, "Bea, Bea Faye, time to come home now." I would be so embarrassed because all the kids would laugh and call my name out the way she called it, "Bea, Bea Faye, time to come home now." Because of this, I didn't long to go to the park much—it became another depressing experience.

Mama loved to fish. She would be gone fishing some evenings when I would get home from school. I was not allowed to let anyone in the house nor was I allowed to go out. "I'm going fishing today and when you get home, you know what you are supposed to do. Don't let me find out that you went outside or let somebody in this house because I will beat you within an inch of your life!"

This I knew would be true. She whipped me so bad one day, about something I didn't do, until I felt numb. The explanation I gave her for not doing what she said I'd done was unacceptable because I was the only one in the house. Therefore, I was lying to her about not knowing where those little blue glasses were; the ones that usually sat on her ceramic poodle. I promise you from that day to this one, I don't ever remember seeing any blue glasses on that poodle. I was whipped for it anyway.

Welted up from numerous hits with a belt, I wondered why she didn't go ahead and kill me. I felt I would have been better off. Anything would be better than this. I am never right; always wrong. I am a liar and a sneaky child. Neither of which I had the guts to do nor become. I was miserable. It would hurt to wear clothes after she whipped me because she drew blood from my skin and that would make me welt up big time. She was mindful not to damage my face— all the damage remained beneath my clothes. I had this infinite fear about going to school and somebody finding out what I looked like under my little Catholic School girl uniform. Then again, sometimes, I wished somebody knew. Yea, Madelene pretty much had complete control over me through her instillation of fear programed inside of me.

My Elementary Years

During my elementary school years, I attended a private Catholic School that was attached to Lainey's church, St. Joseph's. She, I and her brother, Johnny, attended the school and our mothers would take turns taking us and picking us up. I loved the days that Lainey's mom came to pick us up on the bus. She didn't drive so it was always such a cool adventure riding the bus home with her. I would look out the window. Although it was hot, the warm wind blowing on my face felt like freedom. I didn't like the days that Mama came to pick us up because she was always running late. On these days, Johnny would leave the school yard to go and play football at their cousin's house around the corner from the school. Sometimes, his cousins would take him home later. Lainey and I were not allowed to go over to her cousin's house because most of the time there were only boys over there and their cousin, Ben, was a grown man.

I Can't Tell Nobody

On one of those late pick up days, school had been dismissed and the nuns had gone to the convent where they live which was also attached to the school. All the other kids were gone for the day. Lainey and I were the only two children on the campus waiting on my Mom. Ben's wife came around the corner to let me know that she would be taking Lainey and Johnny home because she had to drop something off to their mom.

"Bea, you are welcome to ride with us so that you don't have to sit here by yourself." I was terrified to say yes because if Madelene came looking for me and I wasn't there, I would be dead before Lainey or anybody else found me again.

"No, ma'am, that's ok. My Mama will be here in a minute. She's just probably running a little late."

"Are you sure? I could stop back by the house and call her to ask if it's ok if you want me to?" I was thinking, 'Yea, and you'd have to call her at work and then I'd get beat down for giving you her work number once I got home'. I could hear it now, 'Who told you to give anybody my work number? The people I work for don't want nobody calling they house looking for me. I told you not to give that number to nobody unless it was a real emergency. Your ass can wait on me. I don't care how long it takes. She probably didn't ask you if you wanted to ride anyway, you probably asked her!' I snapped back to reality.

"Uh, no ma'am. I'll be fine. She'll be here soon."

"Well alright, if you're sure you'll be okay. I sure hope she gets here before dark." She took Lainey and Johnny and headed back around the corner. I was praying. I guess I was praying that Mama would come before dark, too. A few minutes after everybody left, Father Mason opened the door to his Parish. I was sitting on a bench adjacent to his front door with tears in my eyes. I guess he could see I was crying from where he was standing.

"Why are you crying?"

"Father, my Mama is running really late today and everyone has left."

"Not everyone has left, I'm here. Come on in and I will give you a glass of water to drink while you wait. Would that be ok'?

As I recall, I'd been going to St. Joseph's since I was in first grade. I knew the Catholic rules, although I was raised Baptist. You did not enter into a priest's parish or a nun's convent because they were like God— sacred and holy. So why was he asking me to come inside and get a drink of water? Now, I was really scared. Scared not to go because he was "Father" and we were all taught to obey him and scared to go because if Mama showed up and found me in any close quarters with a man, she would slit both our throats!

"Ok, I can see you are scared. I'll bring the glass of the water to the door and hand it to you through the screen. Will that be alright?"

"Yes, Father, thank you."

In a child's mind, I was thinking if he handed it to me through the screen, I wouldn't have to go inside. I could see Mama when she drove up and leave him with the water while I ran to the car.

"Good, I'll be right back with the water."

He returned with the water and motioned for me to come to the screen door. Although it was only a few feet away, it seemed as if time stood still until I reached it. He handed the glass of water out of the screen door as I reached for it. When I did, he took his free arm and pulled me into his parish. He sat the glass of water down and put his huge hand over my mouth, he could tell I was about to scream. At the same time, he took his other hand and found the outer lining of my little girl panties and rammed two fingers up my vagina. I couldn't breathe because it hurt so bad. He was red in the face and I was frozen solid. As he withdrew his fingers, he handed me the glass of water and said, "Now, drink so that Christ will wash all your sins away."

My hands were shaking. I could barely get one swallow of the water down. I threw the glass on the floor and ran out. He slammed the door behind me. By the time I reached the bench, I was a wreck. I knew I had to pull it together before Mama drove up. *'Lord, if you are listening, please don't let Mama know, please. She will say it was all my fault and I don't know how that could be. I'm not sure what just happened.'*

Here Comes Mama

Toot, toot, that was the horn on Mama's '57 two-toned Chevy. I ran to the car with a big smile on my face, for once, so happy to see her. "You worked really late today… huh, Mama?"

"Yea and I'm sorry but Mrs. Redford asked me to go over to her sister's house after I finished her house and help her out. I was already tired but we could always use the extra money. How was school?"

"Oh, it was good."

"Hey, wait a minute. Where is Lainey and Johnny? Wasn't I supposed to pick them up, too?"

"Yes, ma'am but Mr. Ben's wife, Ms. Hattie, took them home because she had to drop something off to Mrs. James."

"You know those James' can be so uppity sometimes. Why didn't they ask you if you wanted a ride home instead of leaving you out here all by yourself. I wouldn't have left Lainey or Johnny waiting out here all by themselves."

I didn't know how to tell her that Ms. Hattie did ask me if I wanted a ride but I was afraid to take it.

"Oh well, I'm here now and I'm hungry. Are you hungry?"

"Yes, ma'am."

"Well since I made a little extra change today and I'm too tired to cook, how about we get some fried chicken from the Chicken Coop to take home for supper?" Wow, this meant she was in a good mood. She rarely spent money on eating out.

"For real Mama? For real?"

"I said that's what I was gonna do! Didn't I?"

"Yes, ma'am."

A big smile ran across my face until I felt the pain of Father Mason's fingers again when Mama patted my leg. But I had to keep smiling. She could never find out what happened after school that day. Mama stopped by the Chicken Coop and bought us two-piece chicken meals with cornbread and green beans. The Chicken Coop had the best fried chicken in the world, so it seemed.

When we arrived home, she asked if I had any homework and I told her I had finished it while waiting for her to pick me up. Little did I know, until she pulled out a can to drink with her two pieces, she had stopped somewhere earlier and bought her a six pack of Budweiser. "Them white folks worked me like a runaway slave today, I had to get me some vitamins." (I didn't know for the longest time that Budweiser was not a liquid vitamin. What I did know is by the time she had a couple of cans, she was much calmer, nicer and I felt safe for the time being.)

"Bea, you straighten up the kitchen, take your bath and get in the bed. I'm going to go and take my clothes off and take my bath and go to sleep, I'm tired."

"Yes, ma'am."

I did as she said and straightened up the kitchen, washed the two plates (she did not like eating from a box) and utensils. I swept and mopped the floor and turned the lights off in the kitchen. We didn't have a shower in that old house so mama must have taken a bath in record time because by the time I had finished, she had fallen asleep and was snoring. Thank God! I removed my clothes to get in the bathtub to try and get the "Mason" off me and off my mind. I noticed there was a light pink stain in my underwear and I panicked! If Mama saw that she would swear that I was "fass" and had been fooling around with some little boy. She would hunt him down like a bounty hunter until she found him and Lord only knows what she would do to him after she found him. If I washed them outright, she would become suspicious. I had to think.

Our bathroom was small and I pretended to trip over the stool she always had sitting in there. My panties were in my hands so when

I pretended to trip over the stool, I let them fall out of my hands in to the bathwater. I practiced before I woke her up and told her what happened. I thought she would get up to see if I were lying and proceed to investigate the incident further. But she didn't. She just rolled over and said, "Just wash them out in the bathwater before you get in, then hang them over the washing machine in the kitchen." There was a God.

The next day at school, I never saw Father Mason and I was so glad. From then on out, if Mama was late picking us up, I convinced Lainey that we should wait outside the school gate on the old bus stop bench where the bus didn't stop anymore. That way we could jump right in the car. Most afternoons, Johnny was there with us throwing rocks and teasing us until Mama showed up. It was so funny how she was late almost every other day pre-Mason but since I prayed, she never arrived late again.

I Got the Paddle

Saint Joseph's was closing after my sixth grade year. It cost tuition to attend that school but it was worth it. At least, that's what Mama said. I don't know how much she paid but I did learn a lot. Not that I was so smart but school had become an escape for me, so I loved going. I think what made us studious at St. Joseph's was the discipline.

Sister Mary David did not play. None of the nuns did. If you were tardy or disrespectful, they took care of that right on the spot. They would pull out this huge paddle while you held out your hand.

You would receive two licks and that was your punishment. Your hand would turn blood red and start aching. Whatever you had done wrong, you never repeated it. I remember when I received my first two licks from Sis. Mary David. Mama had made me late that morning. I walked in and class had already begun. In mid-sentence, Sis. Mary David took out her paddle and ask me to step forward. I received my licks and sat down. I felt ashamed and embarrassed all day. The kids never spoke of it or made fun of me because that was against the rules. If a Sister caught you doing such a thing, you would have to hold out your hand, too.

When school was over and Mama came to pick me up, (Mrs. James had come on the bus earlier to pick up Lainey and Johnny because they had doctors' appointments), she noticed that I was nursing my right hand a little.

"What's wrong with your hand?"

"I got the paddle today."

"You got the paddle today for what? What in the hell did you do Bea!"

"I was late." Silence.

"Oh. Well, that couldn't be helped. I ain't going nowhere until I have two cups of coffee so that my bowels can move. They don't take too kindly to you pooping in the toilets while you at work. You'll be fine."

"But it still hurts."

"After all day? Girl, you are so weak and such a whiner. Put some alcohol on it when we get home and toughen up."

I remember thinking about how she didn't care that I was in pain. She didn't care about anything but drinking her two cups of coffee and going to the bathroom before taking me to school. (As an adult, I have refused to pick up any of her bad habits like coffee or cigarettes. Living without motherly love and affection was habit enough for me.)

It was getting close to the end of the year and the Sisters were meeting with parents to suggest alternatives for enrollment since this was the last year St. Joseph's would be open. The other Catholic Schools were too expensive and Mama couldn't afford them. (Lainey and Johnny had a Daddy at home that Mrs. James didn't always run off.) Mr. James enrolled the kids in Perpetual Help Catholic School. I, on the other hand, was enrolled in public school. I was hoping that public school would bring new adventure and new knowledge. Being a top student in Catholic School meant you would not be lost if you ever had to go to a public school. At least, that's what the nuns told our parents. By the time school started the next year, all of us who attended Catholic and had to move on to public school would see how right the nuns were.

Chapter Three
IN THE MIDDLE

What a rude awakening! Public school was nothing like my old school and all the kids sound so unlearned and they are mean. I didn't like it, not one bit. It was foreign to me in every way. There were rules but they were enforced differently. When a student misbehaved, they were given something called a Discipline Slip and sent to the Principal's Office. After receiving three of these slips within a certain time frame, you were suspended and could not return to school for three days. If that ever happened to me in that school, I would not be resurrected on the third day.

7th Grade

I was a great student of course. All my teachers loved me and thought so highly of me. They would express their delight to Madelene on Parent Night. She never seemed phased by their compliments. She would always leave those meetings with a stern, "She better be!"

Unfortunately, the students at Stephens Junior High did not think highly of me at all. They saw me as a threat and a teacher's pet because I was always knowing the right answers to questions and always being called on to explain or read aloud in class. Besides that, I was light skinned and had long thick hair and the girls in this neighborhood couldn't stand that about me, either. You see, at St. Josephs (my elementary school), I was separated from the regular kids in the neighborhood because Mama paid for me to go to private school. Where we lived, most parents could not afford to do that. The public-school kids looked at me as if I thought I was better than they were, although, that was the farthest thing from my mind. I had tried to make friends but ended up with just two friends from my neighborhood. They had attended Catholic schools, too, so we could relate to each other and often complained about this horrible transition. We mainly kept to ourselves so that we wouldn't be bullied or made fun of.

The Bullying Begins

I was the most verbal out of the three of us, so I forced myself to become involved with some extracurricular activities like the academic decathlon. I wanted my friends and me to be recognized as good student examples and friendly. In seventh grade while trying to feel better about this public school transition, the bullying started. I really didn't bother anyone. I stayed in my own little world, inside my own little circle. But since the school was only a mile away from my house, Mama allowed me to walk home.

Most of the rough kids in the neighborhood walked home, too. My only two friends, Lottie and Dee, would walk with me every day until they reached the turn off to their streets, which was before I reached mine. There were three blocks where I walked by myself. One afternoon, on the way home, I noticed a crowd following behind me. A crowd had never followed behind me before. This was all so new to me. I didn't have a clue as to what was about to take place.

One of the girls yelled out, "Hey, Bea Faye or is it Butt Face?" The crowd roared. I kept walking with my head down.

"I heard you called my Mama a bitch!" I would never say those words about anyone's mama. It was bad enough Madelene cussed all the time but I knew I better not cuss and she hear about it.

"I'm sorry, you must be mistaken. I don't know your mother nor do I know you."

"Well, will you listen to that? She's got a white girl voice. No wonder she is always the teacher's flunky."

Another girl chimed in, "Yeah and I bet she thinks she's white, too, just because she has long hair and is light skinned."

There was a little corner store just down the street from my house and that's where all the neighborhood fights took place. We were all approaching the store. The very next moment somebody grabbed my ponytail and pulled my head forward while several other girls took their fists and beat me in my back. This went on for about five minutes. Then, they all ran off laughing so hard they were crying. I continued walking home so glad that Mama had gone fishing for the evening and I would be home by myself. I tried for the life of me to figure out why all these things were happening to me. What had I done except be adopted?

Once again, I could not breathe a word about this to Mama or else she could end up in jail and I could end up an orphan. The bullying and one-sided beat downs went on at least once a week. The entire school would look at me and laugh about what a coward I was. I was in emotional pain and physical pain most of the days of my life while in the middle (middle school). Word had gotten out that I was being jumped on quite often, even Papa knew. Papa had started working late to avoid Mama. He wanted to protect me but there were not enough hours in the day for him to get off work and make it over to the neighborhood in time to put a stop to all of this.

Things slowed down for a while so I thought the coast was clear and they were bored with picking on me. And then it happened. On the walk home one day, an enormous crowd was following me. This was the largest crowd ever since I had been a bully target. I turned around to see if it were any of the regulars but couldn't identify any. This was a new girl. She was an eighth grader with the reputation of being strong and rough. Her name was Katy Evans but everybody called her Choo-Choo because they said once she started beating you up, you would feel like you had been hit by a train.

Choo-Choo was leading the pack. Fear rushed over me and I asked God to just let me go to Heaven based on all the things I had tried to do right. Before we reached the corner store fighting space, Choo-Choo had hit me in my back so hard, it knocked the breath out of me. She was not waiting to reach the store spot. She spoke low but the actual accusation had something to do with me talking about her and her family. Woosh! A blow to my right rib. Woosh! A blow to my left rib. She had beat me all the way to the store spot. That is where I fell to the ground. Motionless, breathless and in great pain. No one stayed to see if I would rise or be able to walk home.

Ms. Addy, a nice lady that lived across the street from the store, was standing on her driveway in tears. She walked over and helped me up and said to wait there so she could give me a ride home. In a car? I was less than three minutes away from the house. I thanked her as I tried to close the door to her car, she had to help me. I managed to unlock the back door and go inside the house. I told myself I would only lie down for a few moments, get up, change my clothes and do my chores. As I laid across my bed with my legs hanging over the side, I cried myself to sleep. Suddenly, I was awakened by the closing of the front door. Madelene! Oh no! I was still in my school clothes and I hadn't done any chores. What was I going to tell her?

"Bea, why you in the bed so early and with your school clothes still on?" Trying to sit straight up, without indicating I was in pain, I told her that we had to run a lot of laps in P.E. because track season is coming up and Coach was pushing everybody to the limit.

"Uh huh. Get up, Gal and take those clothes off so I can wash them." I was thinking that she would leave my room so that I could undress but she stood there.

"Come on now." I slid off the bed and without hesitation I grabbed my right side, a tear fell.

"Take your clothes off, Bea." I disrobed and she examined me from head to toe. She made some Epson Salt bath water and had me to sit down in it up to my neck.

"Who did this to you?"

"Choo-Choo."

"Who in the hell is Choo-Choo?"

"Katy Evans."

"Katy Evans, Wanda Evans' gal?"

"I guess, I'm not sure."

"I know you didn't do anything to that girl or all them other girls you've been letting jump on you on the way home from school. You are too scary for that."

Now I'm thinking if you knew I was being jumped on, why didn't you say something about it? Why didn't you protect me, teach me to fight or something? I let out a loud cry.

"Shut up! Yeah, I knew about the other fights but I didn't say anything because I thought your instinct would kick in to protect yourself. I guess I was wrong. You are not tough like me. I would have been slanging them heifers all over this neighborhood the first time any one of them said anything to me. I think about how hard I've worked to send you to a private school so that you would get a good education. I guess, I never thought you would be smart but weak at the same time. So, I'm going down to Wanda Evans' house and have a talk with her about her Amazon-ass daughter—big as a tree, jumping on you. You sit in this tub until I get back. You hear me?"

"Yes, ma'am."

And sat I did. I sat and I sat and I sat until I started to wrinkle up like Jane Pittman. But if she said not to get out, I better not get out. It felt like she had been gone for hours. I had visions of murder attempts committed by Madelene on Wanda Evans and her daughter running through my mind. Maybe she hadn't come back because she cut Choo-Choo and her Mama up. Madelene always kept a very sharp pocketknife with her. Although, I could not get out of the tub to verify that she took it with her over to the Evans', I knew she did. I finally heard her coming back in the house and boy was I glad.

"You still in the tub?"

"Yes, ma'am."

"Well, you can get out now. We need to talk."

She didn't really sound angry; she sounded different. As a matter of fact, I wasn't afraid about the nature of the talk, which was unusual. I dried myself off, put on my pajamas and met her in the living room. She had a high back gold velvet chair one of the ladies she worked for gave her. She would sit in that chair and drink her coffee, smoke her cigarettes and conduct our little talks.

"Alright, now I am only going to explain this to you one time. Wanda Evans' girl will not be bothering you anymore. Her mother and I came to an understanding. She knows that girl is way too big to be picking on you."

"Thank you, Mama."

Something between a smirk and a smile came across my lips thinking about how Mama had really saved me, maybe.

"Now, don't go thinking you are in the clear

from being bullied, you are not. I talked to Wanda but I did not talk to every momma in this neighborhood and I'm not going to. But what you are going to do is the next time anybody bullies you, you are going to beat the sh--- out of 'em and make them wipe it up with their hands! Do you hear me?"

"Yes, ma'am".

I started feeling sick to my stomach just thinking about such an ordeal. I might as well lay down like a doormat because I couldn't do what she was commanding me to do. I just didn't know how to fight. I had never been taught.

"Because you listen to me and you listen good. If you come home one more time beat up, then I am going to finish beating your ass when you get home!"

My eyes grew two sizes larger that day.

"Am I clear?"

"Yes ma'am, Mama. You're clear."

"Good. Now, I am going to let you slide on mopping the floor tonight because I know you are sore. Go on and do your homework and I will call you for a bowl of stew once it's heated up."

"Yes, ma'am."

She sounded almost human, concerned and perhaps even afraid for me. Was this love? I dare not question it or anything else for that matter. I was only supposed to be seen and not heard.

After homework and stew, I slowly laid down on the less bruised rib and tried to sleep. I looked toward the ceiling in my room where there was a small hole that I imagined would become my escape route one day. *'Lord, if there is a next fight, please let me win so that Madelene won't kill me'.* The window was up and I could hear the quiet sounds of the night. It was hot but after my little prayer, I felt a cool breeze come across my face. I wasn't going to die.

It had been at least a month and all was quiet on the walking home front. I had made at least two more new friends and our little nerd circle was growing. We would have so much fun laughing about things that most of the kids had no idea about. Things like the solar system, propaganda, grey matter, marketing, and all kinds of things that were discussed in our world where everybody felt comfortable and could be themselves.

My friends had reached their turn offs and I was cheerfully walking home when suddenly, I heard a crowd gathering behind me. The sound was so familiar. Whose mama did I call a b---- this time? Who's claimed boyfriend had spoken to me? Or was my hair too bushy or too straight that day? What? It was obvious that the crowd was looking to be entertained at my expense. My memory kicked in concerning what Mama had told me: *"If you come home one more time beat up, then I am going to finish beating your ass when you get home!"* That just could not happen.

A Victory Finally Maybe

The bully this time was a little shorter than me and had a loudmouth. All I knew was her name was Jeanie and she hung around with the tough gang for recognition, I suppose. I allowed her to shout obscenities and push me in my back all the way up to the corner store. Once we reached that store, I lost it! I grabbed her by her neck, threw her on the ground, placed my bony knee in her chest and started beating her in her face while saying, "You are not going to make my Mama kill me! You are not! You understand me? You're not going to make her kill me!" The crowd was shocked into silence.

My fist kept hitting her and hitting her and I didn't feel no ways tired. A couple of the larger girls managed to pull me off her but I could have remained in that victory position a little while longer.

"She's crazy!" somebody from the crowd shouted.

"Let's go!"

Jeanie had a busted lip and had to be helped up off the ground.

"My brother has a gun and he will come after you."

"My Mama has a gun, too, and she don't miss!"

The remainder of the kids giggled at the statement I made and proceeded to walk to their homes.

I couldn't believe I won a fight. I felt like Joe Louis or somebody. A victory had finally come my way. Now, I knew once Mama heard the news, she would be so proud of me. She would feel like she had a smart girl and a tough girl, too. Nothing could have been better than the feeling of victory on that day. I could not wait to get home and tell Mama the news.

I ran inside the house yelling, "Mama, guess what?"

"What?"

"I had a fight today and I won! I won, Mama!"

"I guess you can count that little Jeanie girl as a victory although, she is smaller than you. I guess you take a win wherever you can get it." I stood stunned.

The joy of victory left. But I can say I never had another physical fight after that day. Showing those girls that I was not afraid to protect myself anymore caused them to move on to their next target. I guess Mama is right, sometimes.

8th Grade

Eighth grade was a breeze. By now, I was established as a smart kid and a thespian. Although my career goals were set for public relations (PR), I enrolled in a speech class. It helped to develop my public speaking skills which I knew I would need later for PR presentations. Ms. Catlin, my Speech teacher, introduced me to the spirit of competition in that class and I loved it. Besides composing speeches and developing presentations, there were speech tournaments. I wasn't too sure about entering at first but Ms. C. (Ms. Catlin) said I would be a first-place winner in dramatic interpretation because of my gift of memorization and presentation.

My First and My Last Forensic Tourney

I remember my first tournament. It was held inside a high school on the north side of town where most of the rich people lived. I was in awe of the place. It was three stories high with tons of classrooms and a cafeteria as large as a first- class gym. I was so lost. We were all given the time of our events and the rooms in which we would be competing.

At first, I felt like I would never find my room on time. Good thing that the host school had other students direct us to the correct rooms so that we would not be late. If we were late, we could not enter the room. I made it right before they shut the door and put the DO NOT DISTURB sign on the outside. Ms. C. was in the Coach's Lounge where the coaches patiently waited on individual scores from each event their teams had entered. At the end of the day, everyone assembled in the cafeteria to see who placed in the different categories. If your school gained the most points in every category your school entered, that school would receive a huge trophy. Individual winners would receive a medal.

I was so used to having Ms. C. around to encourage me until for a few moments, I felt as if I couldn't do this. Then the reminder came. You have done this already Bea. Remember Bible Storytelling? Memory verse? Winning!? Yes, I can do this!

"Bea Faye, Stephens Junior High."

I stood up and walked to the front of the room. I gave my introduction and proceeded to present a dramatic interpretation of *I Know Why the Cage Bird Sings* by Maya Angelou. You were only allowed seven minutes. I began to feel myself rushing a bit but according to the timekeeper in the back of the room, I finished in six minutes and fifteen seconds. Whew! I was nervous and I felt myself perspiring. In that classroom were kids that entered thespian competitions all the time and won. You knew who they were—they never spoke or smiled. They were so serious.

Once my session was over, I headed back down to the cafeteria where I sat at our school table. A few of the other students were already there talking about their experiences. All of us felt as if we did alright but we probably would not be taking home that huge trophy, not this time, anyway. With everyone reassembled, the Awards Ceremony was about to begin. There were only five of us who were entered in this tournament but Ms. C. made us feel as if we were twenty-one strong. She was such a great and inspiring teacher. If I ever changed my mind about PR and decided to go into education, I would want to be just like Ms. C.

The announcer stepped to the podium, "In the Novice Poetry Category in third place." Nobody from our school had entered Novice Poetry. Jackie was entered in Solo Humorous Interpretation. Mary Jane was entered in Solo Pantomime. Roger was entered in Impromptu Speaking. Karen was entered into Solo Serious Interpretation and I was in Dramatic Interpretation.

There were so many categories and it was getting late. Ms. C. stated on the permission slip that the bus would return to the campus by six pm. They were just getting around to our categories and it was already five-thirty. There was no way to call Madelene and let her know we would be getting back late. I knew she would be on campus at exactly six pm waiting for me to step off that bus. I was becoming terrified at what she might do if I arrived late. But what could I do? It is not my fault that the event ran behind. *'Oh Lord, please don't let her hit or cuss me in front of my teacher and classmates. Please?'* I was in such deep thought that I never heard my name called. Everybody was screaming and jumping up and down.

"Bea, you won First Place for Dramatic Interpretation."

"I what? I did?"

"Bea, go and get your medal!"

Ms. Catlin was beaming. I recall how special I felt that day. My very first time in a school competition and I won First Place. I will never forget that feeling. Overall, we did not do so bad for our first tournament. Everyone placed either second or third. I was the only one who placed first.

The bus arrived back to the school campus around seven-thirty pm, one hour and a half later than projected. And there was Madelene, standing outside the car with a cigarette in her hand, fuming. Everyone was so proud and happy about our accomplishments so they didn't notice Madelene had smoke coming from her ears. Ms. Catlin just HAD to say something to her. *'Lord, please remember what I asked you to do for me.'*

"Mrs. Faye, you have an extraordinarily talented daughter. This was her first tournament and all of the kids placed in their categories but Bea, she won First Place!"

Madelene just smirked and said, "Thank you."

Ms. C. could tell she was upset about something and couldn't figure out what it was. I knew what it was. She drove home in silence. I wanted to show her my medal but I knew that now was not the time. Once at home, she remained quiet as I went about my usual routine of taking off dirty clothes, putting them in the dirty clothes basket, picking up the kitchen, sweeping and mopping. Then, on to my bath and pajamas. As I was coming out of the bathroom, Madelene spoke, "We need to talk."

Same Old, Same Old

I knew that meant instead of watching television or curling up with a book, I had to meet her in the living room while she sat in that gold high back velvet chair and I on the green ottoman.

"Mama, before we talk can I at least show you the medal I won?"

"I don't give a damn about no medal. I am upset about you not getting to that school 'til nighttime. And I'm mad as hell that your teacher kept you out until all hours of the night just for a medal. You are not going to another one of those damn things. Anything could happen— all girls and one boy plus a grown man on that bus. You all could have been raped. Good things don't happen in the dark. If it's going to be night every time you get back here, then you can't go!"

"But mama,"

"But mama nothing, you heard me. Now, carry your ass to bed and I don't want to hear nothing else about no tournament."

Same old, same old. Everything that God meant for my good, Madelene made it out to be bad. On Monday, I told Ms. Catlin that I couldn't be a part of the team anymore because we had arrived later than the permission slip stated.

"Did you explain to your Mother that we as the Coaches have no control over when the tournament ends?"

"Yes, ma'am." I lied.

"Perhaps if I scheduled a meeting with her to explain how these…"

"I'm sorry, Ms. C. Unless they start at eight am and I am home by four pm, I cannot go. I'm so sorry."

"Me too Bea. Me too; but don't give up. I am sure I can enter you in a tournament that will get you back by four o'clock."

"That would be great Ms. C.!"

She walked away with a determined step. It didn't matter, Madelene ruled again. This time, taking me out of something I really loved and had fun doing. It felt like I was pre-destined to live a miserable life.

Back at home, I finished my chores, took my bath and stayed in my room the rest of the evening, there was nothing left to say. The remainder of my eighth-grade year in middle school went rather slowly because I couldn't participate in anything. Decathlon was over. I couldn't go to any more tournaments. Gospel choir was full and besides, I couldn't sing so it was back to closed in boundaries.

How Do I Believe in Myself?

Then one day, Dee, my best friend, sparked an idea. She said that they were having cheerleader tryouts and if we made the team, we would be on the B Squad in high school next year.

"Come on Bea, let's do it!"

"I don't know about all that Dee, I'm not athletic and I can't do the splits!"

"I will help you learn. Coach Barber likes you because you are the fastest runner in our P.E. class. I bet she would let us practice during class."

"But what if I make the team? Mama would never allow me to be on it anyway."

"Why?"

"Because the games are held at night and football involves boys!"

"Oowee, don't it though!"

"Girl, hush!"

"Then don't make the team but at least you would have had the experience of trying out. Besides, you would have tried out with me, your best friend. So, what do you say?"

"I guess. But you and nobody else can tell my Mama about this."

"You know I'm not; I like living." We both laughed.

Tryouts were only a week away now. Coach Barber had allowed Dee and I to practice the last fifteen minutes of class every day for the last three weeks. We had the audition routine perfected and felt ready.

Lottie, our quietest friend, was a big support on the day of the try outs. She had water and snacks and pom-poms. We had to audition in groups. Dee and I were placed in Group Four, the beginner's group, so we didn't feel intimidated. The Coach called out Group Four. We ran out excited and yelling and screaming and Dee, who is hilarious, did a somersault upon her entry. I had no intention of being a cheerleader but I was doing this for Dee and to gain some future brownie points in case I wanted to try out for something else once we were in high school. Our routine was going well until at the very end, I turned the wrong way and messed up the pattern. Everyone was laughing at me and chanting, "Butt face Faye, you turned the wrong way."

I just walked off before we were dismissed to leave the floor. I felt as if I messed it up for Dee and I didn't want to face her.

"Bea, we did it!"

"Did what, Dee? All I did was make you look bad by turning the wrong way?"

"No, you did not make me look bad. I knew I would not be selected for the squad even before I started preparing for tryouts."

"Huh? Why did you try out then?"

"Because I could. Sometimes Bea, you must believe in yourself enough to take a risk to prove to yourself that humiliation will not stop you but it's determination that drives you. It's not what others think of us. It is what we think of us."

Dee was right. It was what we thought of ourselves. My only question was: what if you did not know what to think of yourself? Especially, when you had been told all your life that if you were not watched, commanded, and fearful you would not make it in this world... You would only be the reflection of someone who gave birth to you that and that person was bad. I had tried to think of myself as pretty, important, smart and gifted but it seemed as if my thoughts were always so short-lived. If I was not being bullied at school, I was being torn down at home. My Papa was the only parent that made me feel special and full of worth. He was always so proud of everything I accomplished and even if I did not accomplish anything, he was still proud of me. He always told me that.

On the other hand, Madelene never spoke anything positive into my life. She made me afraid of her, afraid of love, afraid of people…afraid of everything. I was always threatened into what she told me to do. Then, I was punished, if according to her, I did it wrong. I felt like I just didn't matter to her. Never a 'I love you', or 'Mama is so proud of you'. Nor did she ever even say 'how pretty and cute you look today'. Not a word. When a child is small that is the time you begin to instill in them "positive things" not negative ones. Your influence on them will follow them, guide them, or damage them for the rest of their lives.

In The Middle

It took me a long time to think about myself as a wonderful person, an attractive person and worth so much to God as well as to this world. It just did not happen while I was stuck in the middle. In the middle? I was in the middle of trying to understand why Madelene was the way she was. I had heard in Sunday School that every good and perfect thing comes from the Lord. Did that include her? I suppose it did but perhaps she missed God's lesson in the "Love is patient, love is kind" episode in the Bible. I wasn't sure what every single scripture meant then and I surely don't know now, either. But at that time in my younger years, the part about love is long suffering, I figured it meant I would suffer a long, long time under Madelene's love.

Should love really cause suffering though? I guess, if you look at what Jesus did for us on the cross. It was suffering because of how much He loved us. But I am not Jesus and there are days that I'm not sure whether I love Madelene that much. Okay, so that sounds bad. It's just that it seems so confusing to me for someone to be your parent but thinks the worst of you. Or better yet, makes you think the worst of yourself. The truth is, if something is spoken into your spirit consistently, after a while, you start to believe it. I was brought up to believe that your Mama was always right and you had to respect and do what she said no matter what.

At the church, there was a lot of emphasis placed on honoring your mother and your father so that your days would be long upon this earth. I probably don't have this exactly right but what if you honor your mother and she still threatens to shorten your life upon this earth? As a child, you should want to obey your parent because it is one of God's commandments. In my case, it was one of my ways to stay out of the obituaries.

I often tried to identify the type of love Madelene had for me. Looking around at other children and their mothers, mine seemed so different. You could see mothers holding the hands of their children, helping them cross the street. Madelene forbid me to want to go across the street. They would hug their children, brush their hair out of their faces, kiss them on the forehead. They would laugh with them, play with them and encourage them. Other mothers would inspire their children to believe they could become whomever they wanted to become. Madelene would command and demand who I was and who I never would become. Most of the time, I would imagine running away from home or one of my siblings coming to rescue me. The restrictions and fear of how I was raised caused me to have an active imagination. Between God and that imagination, I could go anywhere in my mind and become anyone I wanted with no restraints. I was safe and secure when I imagined.

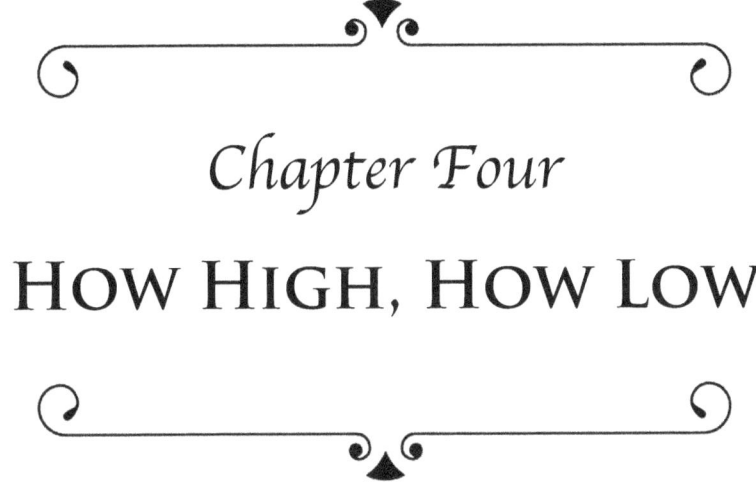

Chapter Four
HOW HIGH, HOW LOW

Something happened to me between the summer after eight grade and the fall of ninth grade—boys. Although, Madelene told me that I was not pretty, I was her little flat nosed baby and no one would ever love me except her, I wanted to take a shot at having a boyfriend; behind her back, of course.

9th Grade

In my neighborhood, there was a recreational center where all the teens hung out on Friday nights at the teen dances. At that time in my life, it seemed as if the whole world of teenagers could go to those dances, minus one—me. Even Lottie's Mama let her go and they were Pentecostal!

There was this boy I liked who lived in our neighborhood. He was in the tenth grade at the high school. He would always attend those dances at the Center because he was quite popular. He had spoken and smiled at me a couple of times when I ran into him at the corner store. I remember thinking how handsome he was and how I would be so proud to be his girl one day.

A Chance at A Dance

It was Friday and I was on my way to class when one of my books fell from my arms. Guess who picked it up for me? Yep, my future husband. (Funny how girls always thought in terms of long-range relationships.) His name was Morris Chancy. He bent over with ripped muscles and masculinity and handed me my AP English book. He then smiled and said, "Hope I see you at the Center tonight Bea" as he walked off. I took that statement as an invitation that I had to be at that dance tonight. My brain was working overtime trying to devise a plan to be in attendance. I recalled that Mrs. Ford, who knew my Mom, was over the community volunteer group for Booker T. Washington High School. She oversaw creating opportunities for students in high school to build their community portfolios that would attract college scholarships. I didn't know if she had any pull to place me at the Center but it would not hurt to ask. I knocked on the door to Mrs. Ford's office.

"Come on in, the door's open."

"Mrs. Ford?"

"Well, will you look at you? You are growing like a weed, Bea. How 's Madelene doing?" "Haven't talk to her in a while."

"She's fine."

"So, how can I help you?"

"I was interested in volunteering at the neighborhood center, you know the one on Easter Street?"

"Yes, I do and I think that's a great idea. I know the Director over there and she is always short on volunteers, especially on Friday nights when she is stuck with all those teens at the dance." (BINGO!) "If you volunteer more than once and in different venues, it will look really good in your college portfolio."

"Yes, ma'am. That's what my 9th Grade Counselor told me."

"Let me see now, I have the volunteer forms for the Center here somewhere." *('Please let her find them, Lord.')*

"Oh, here they are. Now all you must do is get Madelene to sign this form and you will be set up to help Ms. Topper at the Center next Friday night, ok?" (NEXT FRIDAY, OH NO! Morris was expecting me to show up tonight.)

"Mrs. Ford, is there any way I could begin volunteering at the Center tonight? I just feel like the sooner I get started with my community service work, the better it will look."

"I don't know Bea. We must have parent permission on file at least one week in advance."

"Maybe you could call my Mom and ask her permission that I start tonight instead of next week.?"

"That may be an option. Wait here a moment and let me check with my Supervisor."

(Oh, my goodness, I cannot believe I am going through all this just to be in the same room with Morris. If Mama ever found out that this was all about a boy, I would be circumcised. Wait, can girls be circumcised? Small beads of sweat started to appear around my hair line. I didn't know what the outcome of all of this would be but I just felt as if Morris was worth it.)

"Alright Bea, I will give Madelene a call and ask her permission to allow you to start this evening. I called Ms. Topper while I was in with the Boss and she is more than ready for your help. I will go through your files and find Madelene's work number and give her a call. When she gives me permission, I will send for you so that I can speak to you concerning the responsibilities of volunteering."

"Yes, ma'am." I almost skipped out of her office.

My Mom would probably say yes because Mrs. Ford was over her Women's Ministry group at our church. Although behind closed doors Madelene cussed, smoked, drank beer, threatened, and whipped me when she felt like it, the church folks never knew it. They just knew she never smiled and that they should never cross her. Mrs. Ford had gotten past all of that with Mama because they worked on a project together once. Mama even invited her over to the house. Mrs. Ford, in turn, invited Mama to her house and she went. They became friends, not close, just friends. A big smile came across my lips: I was going to the Community Center Dance, not to dance but to be there for Morris. The time seemed to pass so slowly before Mrs. Ford sent for me to come back to her office. This is it—my ticket to normalcy, to be among the good, the bad and the ugly. I was excited beyond reason. I held my head up as if I had been elected student body president.

"Hi, Mrs. Ford."

"Come on in, Bea." She didn't sound like she had good news for me about volunteering at the Center.

"I called Madelene and she said she would allow you to volunteer but only until nine o'clock. That poses a problem because the teen dance is not over until ten and that is when Ms. Topper needs you the most, when the dance is over. The only thing I can do is ask Ms. Topper if she would be willing to let you volunteer under those restrictions."

I stood deadpan-faced without speaking a word. I should have known Madelene would never let me be free.

"Should I wait until you have an answer from Ms. Topper?"

"What about your class? She may not be able to answer the phone right away. I would hate for you to fall behind because of a phone call."

"Oh no, ma'am. I am the Student Assistant in that class because I am already ahead a credit. I won't miss anything."

"Very well then, I will see if I can reach her as soon as I fax some forms over to the NAACP."

She had no idea that I had not planned on leaving that office until Ms. Topper said it would be alright if I left the Center by nine. The dance started at seven right at nightfall and was over by ten. Three hours long, that was it, just three hours? But because of this woman who became my Mother, I had to return home an hour earlier?

At least thirty minutes had passed and Mrs. Ford had not returned to her desk with an answer. The bell rang for my seventh period class, the last class of the day. I am sure my teacher, Dr. Willis, wouldn't mind letting me stay in Mrs. Ford's office until I received my answer. Having the same class twice, as a student, then as an assistant, I was already caught up on my work. I just needed to let him know where I was so I would not be counted absent. I ran out of her office and down the hallway just before the tardy bell rang. Dr. Willis was standing at the door preparing to close it. I explained to him what was going on and he was so understanding. He was kindhearted like Papa. He reminded me of him and I know I admired him because of his heart. His care and compassion to see to it that every child had an opportunity to attend college was always a priority.

"No problem Bea. I am proud of you preparing for college in your Freshman year. That's what it's going to take, preparation and hard work. Did you finish the essay on Amistad?"

"Yes, sir. It's already in the completed work folder."

"I should have known that it was already there. You are one of my brightest Black History students and I appreciate all the good work you do in my class."

"Thank you, sir." (Can I go now. Ms. Topper may have said yes by now.)

"No problem Bea, have a good weekend."

Have a good weekend? That meant I didn't have to go back to his class so I would leave school early. I needed the extra time to decide what I was going to wear to this dance to impress Morris, if only for two hours. Approaching Mrs. Ford's office, I heard her talking to her Secretary, who had been at lunch earlier, through the outside of her office door.

"Poor kid, I don't have the heart to tell her that Topper said unless she can stay until ten, she won't need her services. She said cleaning up after the dances is beginning to take a toll on her health. There are at least 10 volunteers standing around basically doing nothing except socializing, passing out snacks and dancing. But as soon as ten o'clock comes, the volunteers have vanished except for maybe one or two. She really needs Bea to stay."

"You know Bea's Mom, so why don't you offer to take Bea home by ten? Show up around nine-forty and wait on her so you can escort her home. Perhaps that may be how she will have a chance to stay the extra hour."

"You obviously don't know Madelene Faye! She would not trust that child riding home with God— let alone me! I am just going to have to tell Bea the truth."

I opened her office door.

"It's alright, Mrs. Ford. I heard everything and I know you tried." A huge tear ran down my cheek.

"I am so sorry Bea. I wish there was more I could do."

"It's ok. Thanks anyway." I walked back out that door thinking what I had done wrong to be defeated at every attempt, at every turn to have a normal teenaged life—one without fear, without obsession or isolation. *'Lord what did I do?!'*

The weekend came and went. Mama told me her reasoning for me coming back from the Center by nine. "Nice Christian girls don't hang out all hours of the night. That's just inviting these little boys around here to take advantage of you. Don't you understand that? If you hang around with hoes, then everybody will think you are a hoe. You are not embarrassing me—hard as I work to give you a good life. I am not having you turn out like your real Mama."

"I wasn't going to hang out, Mama. I was going to help out."

"I guess you think I'm stupid. You started menstruating two years ago when you were in seventh grade. That means you have started to like boys. Let me tell you something young lady, ain't nobody—and I do mean nobody—is going to love you like I am, so you might as well get boys off your mind. All they want to do is kiss on you and get you worked up and give you a baby. I am telling you right now, if you come up with a baby and you ain't married, all your shit is going to be right out there in that ditch— and you with it. I am not raising no hoes! And you are not getting married until you finish college, have a good teaching job and can live on your own. I don't ask nobody for nothing and you are not going to ask nobody for nothing, either. God bless the chile who's got his own! And next time you think you want to volunteer at the Center, it better not be at night! Now that's all I have to say about that."

I couldn't look in Morris' direction after that. Within myself, I thought I had let him down. The fact that he said he would see me there, to me meant that he wanted to see me there. That's why I tried so hard. Time, rumor and gossip proved me wrong on all counts. The buzz around the school was that he and Felicia Stone kissed that night at the dance and now they were girlfriend and boyfriend.

I was beginning to feel like what Mama said was true. Nobody would ever love me except her. I know I was young and so unwise but ever since she made Papa stay away, there was nobody to love me except her and she had a strange way of doing it. She never failed to tell me repeatedly that I was not pretty or cute—that I belonged to her and I was her little flat nose baby that she kept alive.

"I don't need you to go around thinking you cute or something at that high school. You would just be setting a trap for yourself. I know you are beginning to see that I am always right. You have long hair and light skin and the girls can't stand that. Next thing you know, you'll be getting beat up again and I'll have to cut somebody next time. Then, if you think you're cute, the boys will think you are flirting with them and they will try to blow in your ear and stick their tongues in your mouth. Once they do that, you will become pregnant and I already told you what would happen to you if you did. So that's my talk on boys, leave them alone. Ain't none of them no good. They are all dogs, sniffing under your dress…trying to lay you down. All they do is become dirty old men who force their way through everything just because they think they are stronger than you. None of them will EVER be stronger than me."

This talk sounded like it was more about her than about me. I'm not sure. All I knew was, I better stick to the rules and not end up in the ditch in the front of my house.

My Sophomore Year

One of my high school highs was in my sophomore year; I tried out for the drill team. I not only made the team but was voted in as 2nd Captain for the team. Now, I know you are wondering how Madelene allowed me to be on a drill team— a team that had to attend every football game at night when she held such tight reins on me. Stay with me. The year prior to drill team, Mama had divorced Papa, not long after the skillet incident.

Here's what happened: Papa came home one night quite intoxicated. He hadn't been home in a while but Mama knew where he had been. Papa had been staying with a younger woman on the other side of town because Mama was always kicking him out. He felt frisky this one night when he came home. He tried to get her to sleep with him; she was not having that.

"You my wife, Maddy. Come on Baby, give Papa some loving."

"You better take your hands off me. How dare you come here with that husband privilege in your voice?" "You been laying up with that hoe for weeks and now you come over here as if I'm supposed to roll over and gap my legs."

"Damn right! You still my wife and I have the right to what I need."

I saw a huge thunderstorm coming in Madelene's eyes.

"You better get out of my face and go somewhere and sleep it off."

"What you gone do? Huh? What you gone do, Maddy?"

Mama walked off, like a dummy, he followed her. She always kept an iron skillet on top of our gas stove. He walked behind her. Once in the kitchen, Papa went around the other side of the secondhand kitchen table to get in front of her as if he were going to push her out of the kitchen. When he did, she reached for that iron skillet and hit Papa so hard with her left hand until the impact of his body knocked the kitchen door off its hinges. Papa was laid out on the back door as if it were a stretcher out in the back yard. I screamed. She gave me an evil look, placed the skillet back on the stove and dialed zero.

"I have a drunk husband who fell out the back door. He's not moving, come get him."

I didn't know whether Papa was alive or dead. I was crying asking Mama if she was going to just leave him laying out there in his underwear like that.

"The ambulance people will get him. Let me know when they get here. I'm going back and lay down."

After that, Papa went to the hospital, recovered, picked up his clothes and other belongings from the house and left. She had the lawyer she worked for to draw up the divorce papers and that was that.

What happened shortly after that I would not have believed until I saw it with my own eyes. Mama was spending time with a man. I don't know when or where she met this man but I knew he didn't live in town. Mama would call him her "fishing buddy", Mr. Naylor. She would only speak to me about him when he was coming to town to take her fishing. She said she liked going fishing with him because he had a boat. He was a retired military guy and from the way she spoke of him, he had money. That explained everything. During one of our talks she made a statement, "If a man is going to lay in my bed, he better be ready to put some money in my purse. Ain't nothing for free."

I had no idea as to how far Mr. Naylor traveled but he always seemed to show up on a Friday not leaving town until sometime on Monday. Thus, the drill team participation privilege. Most of the games were on Fridays and rather than have me home alone most of the night, she allowed me to go to the games via drill team. I felt almost grown. Practicing with the band, dancing on the field, it was great, for a while.

My First Kiss

There were only two away games a year. I missed the first one because I was sick with the flu. The second one rolled around in October. Mr. Naylor was supposed to come down so they could take one last fishing trip before the cold weather set in. The town we went to was not that far away, I can't remember the name of it now but after the away games, we would come back to campus early enough to have a victory dance. We had those when we were in town, too— I just was not allowed to stay. Since I knew she was going fishing, I made plans to attend this one. They were always over by eleven-thirty and Dee, who was in the band, always stayed and her mom picked her up when it was over. Tonight, she would give me a ride home as well.

At school, I had been passing notes back and forth to Timmy Shye who was a section leader in the band. Dee was instrumental in introducing us. When he asked if I was staying after the game for the victory dance, I said yes. I was anxious to get back to start dancing and having fun. The bus with the drill team members pulled up right behind the band bus. I lingered a little until I saw Timmy get off the bus. He headed toward me and we started smiling at each other until we were standing face-to-face. He touched my hand. Something ran through me. We walked to the cafeteria hand in hand, like a couple. Timmy was funny, polite, smart and really was a great dancer and— he was white. I was burning up in my drill team uniform from dancing so much but it was so worth it.

Around eleven-fifteen, the teachers and parent chaperones started picking up cups and plates and heading kids toward the door. It was time for me to find Dee. It turns out she was in the band hall clowning around making everybody laugh.

"Dee, it's almost eleven-thirty. Let's go."

"I'll be there in a few minutes. You know my Mom's car so, just let her know I'm on my way."

"Okay." Timmy had been by my side the whole time.

"I'll walk you out."

"Thanks, you are really kind."

"And you are really pretty." Then he leaned over and kissed me on my mouth. I screamed, slapped him, and ran outside. He stood there in shock, not knowing what went wrong. He must have told Dee because she came out to see what was wrong with me.

"Bea, what happened? Did Timmy hurt you because if he did, I'll..."

"Oh Dee, it's worse than that. He made me pregnant."

"WHAT! When did this happen, where?"

"Right now, inside. He kissed me and now I'm pregnant and Mama is going to throw me and all of my things in the ditch that's in the front of the house and…"

"Whoa, wait a minute. You said Timmy kissed you and now you're pregnant?"

"Uh huh."

"Bah, ha, ha, ha, ha!" Dee began to laugh hysterically.

"I thought you were my friend. Here I stand in a world of trouble with no place to live once Mama finds out and all you can do is laugh."

"Bea, forgive me but this is too funny." Anger was rising in me.

"What's funny about this Dee? Tell me what's funny about it!"

"Girl, I don't know who gave you your lesson on the birds and the bees but I assure you, a kiss cannot make you pregnant."

"But that is what Mama has always told me. She warned me that if I let a boy kiss me, I would get pregnant." "No disrespect, but your Mama lied!"

"She-e lied??"

"Yes, girlfriend. I know you don't take health until next semester but go and borrow the health book from Mr. Lancaster. There is a section in there on sex education and the reproductive system. It will explain in scientific terms what takes place to conceive a child and it's not a kiss on the lips! Come on, there's my Mama."

I was furious—ashamed that here I was a top scholar, yet, the truth about what really goes on in my body was a mystery to me. Madelene withheld the truth from me as another one of her control methods. I was so out done. As we were pulling out, Madelene was pulling in. I was scared for a split second, then angry again. Dee's mother stopped beside our car and told Madelene that she was picking the girls up from the victory dance and that she would bring me home. Madelene was angry because she didn't know I was going to the victory dance. (She was supposed to be fishing.)

"That's so nice of you Mae but I'll take Bea from here. I was just running a little late, that's all."

Dee looked at me and rolled her eyes because she knew Madelene was lying and that she was not supposed to be here at all. I left from Dee's car and went over to mine.

"Ok, Madelene. But any time you are running late let me know and I'll be glad to pick the girls up."

"Okay, thanks."

I knew I was going to be lectured, slapped, cussed out, whatever. I didn't care. I was so angry about the nonsense she planted in me until I could have spit nails.

"What are you doing at a damn victory dance? You know I don't allow you to go to those worldly things. You went without my permission and that's the same as lying to me." I thought to myself, just like you lied to me.

"We will talk about this when we get home."

I remained silent. Once inside the house, the phone rang. It was Mr. Naylor. She took the phone in her bedroom and closed the door. I could hear her saying mean things to him like she used to say to Papa. I took off my drill team uniform and started my bath. I wasn't sure whether I was going to get beat while wet or after I dried off. I waited. She was still talking. I had to go ahead and take the bath because if the water became cold and I had to add hot water again she would complain. I finished, dressed for bed, and waited by her gold high back chair. My anger had subsided and I begin to weep.

I must have looked like a crazy person to Timmy, slapping him after he kissed me. I felt sorry for myself. So smart; yet, so dumb. I waited almost an hour; it was almost one in the morning. Sleep was beginning to set in and I was bobbing back and forth on that ottoman. She steps to the door of her bedroom with a half-smile on her face and the phone still up to her ear. In a semi-whisper she says, "Bea, go ahead and get in the bed, we'll talk tomorrow." Tomorrow never dawned on the situation because at six on that Saturday morning, she was waking me up.

"Listen Bea, I'm going fishing with Mr. Naylor. I will be back sometime tonight. You know what your Saturday chores are and I expect them to be done when I get back, understand?"

"Yes ma'am." I thought quickly.

"Oh Mama, can I go to the library once I am finished with everything? I want to get a head start on a project for next week."

"You mean the one next to the elementary school?"

"Yes, ma'am."

"Yes, you can go to that one but don't lie to me and end up at the one downtown."

"Oh no ma'am, Mama." (I can't lie to you like you lied to me.) "It's the one right down the street."

"Now you make sure you take your key and lock the house up. Don't stay down there no longer than an hour and a half, you hear me?"

"Yes, ma'am."

I heard a car drive up. All her fishing gear was at the door and she was dressed and ready to go.

"Bye, Mama."

I Just Didn't Know

Going to the library was another one of my escapes, so I couldn't wait to get there. The first stop was the card catalogue. Let's see, the Reproductive System. It turns out there were several books on the shelves concerning the matter. Finding a nice cozy spot in a corner, I grabbed two books off the shelf and began to read. Time escaped me because the more I read, the more informed I became. Anger began to swell inside me again thinking about all the lies she had told me about getting pregnant from a kiss. I felt so stupid. I decided I would never feel that uninformed again, about anything. Whatever she told me, whether it was about family, friends, school, whatever, I was going to research it and that was final. Without realizing it, I had been at the library four hours. Placing the books back and going over the mental notes I made in my head, I held my head up high as I walked out the door. I had this grand notion that she may beat me but now she could not fool me.

It was late night and Mama had not returned home yet. She never really stayed away this long for fear I would be doing something wrong. It was almost midnight when I heard the back door unlock. She was dragging her fish bucket and sliding her ice chest in the house. Getting out of bed, I ran in the kitchen where she stood gleaming over her catch.

"Look Bea. Look at what I caught while out there on Mr. Naylor's boat." I looked in her long ice chest and saw a fish the entire length of the chest.

"Whoa, what kind of fish is that?"

"It's a sheep head. It has real teeth like a human, see."

Picking up that fish, which looked like it was almost my height, and opening its mouth was scary.

"Look, come in a little closer. He's dead, he won't bite you."

I walked in a little closer and saw that the fish had teeth like a person, just like she said. I remained silent. It was Saturday night a little after midnight and she asked me if I wanted to stay up and watch her "gut" him. Tired from reading and remembering so much, I really didn't want to but I was not allowed to tell her no.

"Ok, I will."

As she went through the process of how to clean this fish step by step, sleep was trying to hold me captive. I knew if I fell asleep while she was talking to me that meant I disrespected her, so I kept trying to stay awake.

"Girl, go ahead and get in the bed. You are sitting up here falling asleep.

"Yes, ma'am." She did not have to tell me twice. I could care less about fishing or her massive catch. I just wanted to be someplace else— live with somebody else. I wanted to escape so that she would not be in control anymore.

Sunday morning showed up in a hurry and the Sunday routine began. Wash up, eat breakfast, get dressed, go! Strangely enough, I couldn't hear Mama stirring at all. I peeped in her room and saw that she was still asleep. Should I wake her up, leave her alone, what? I stood near her bedside and spoke soft and low, "Mama, Mama wake up. It's almost time to go to church." Rolling over, still sleepy she tells me she is too tired to go today and to call Mrs. Niece to see if I could ride with her.

I felt almost grown, going to church without her. Mrs. Niece was more than glad to swing by and pick me up. So, church it was— without Mama. YEAH! I felt like I had been born again for real— walking in church that Sunday. Not having to walk two feet behind my Mama and wait for her to point where she wanted me to sit. I was in high school now and I could handle where to sit all by myself and I did. When church service was over, Mrs. Niece called my Mama to ask her if I could join, she and her family for lunch. Of course, the answer was no because she had gotten up by then and cooked lunch for us and I was going to eat what she cooked. I thanked Mrs. Niece just the same as I got out of her car and walked up to the porch of our house.

Mama was standing there and waved goodbye and yelled, "Thank You." Once inside the house she accused me of begging Mrs. Niece to let me eat with them just because we were running low on food. First, I had no idea we were running low on food; I never asked those type questions. All I knew was that I had to eat what she fixed. I remained silent because if I said anything that meant I was talking back and I would get slapped for that.

"You don't know how hard it is for me, Bea. Trying to make ends meet, take care of the both of us, working two jobs. Sometimes the money just doesn't fall in place like it should. But listen to me" (pointing her finger in my face, here we go), "don't you ever leave God out of your life!" (Huh?) "You can't do nothing without Him. He has taken care of us many of day when you didn't know what was going on." (Like I don't know now?) "Our lights have been turned off. He sent someone to turn them back on. I've been down to my last dime but He stepped right in on time. I don't know what I would do without Him. I just don't know." She began to sob uncontrollably.

I had never seen this side of her. She was always rough and tough and mean. Now, she was crying like Choo-Choo had hit her dead in her heart or something. I didn't know what to think. We had never hugged or touched before—that I could remember—but I did place my hand on her shoulder and said, "Don't worry Mama, it will be alright."

"Oh, I know it will, that's why I work so hard to make sure you get a good education, go to college, get a good teaching job and make something out of yourself. I don't want you to work like I have to work. Barely making ends meet from paycheck to paycheck. I just want better for you, Bea. God can give you better."

That was the kindest thing that had ever been spoken to me by my Mama. She was right about God—I couldn't afford to leave Him out of my life. What revelations. I found out where babies come from for real and saw my Mama cry—all within one weekend. Knowing what I know now about boys and babies, I was keeping my eye out for that first non-impregnated kiss.

My Junior Year

Junior year was rather uneventful. Lottie wasn't hanging around with Dee and me as much as she used to. I quit the drill team after the information about my not knowing that I couldn't get pregnant from a kiss surfaced. I became a walking plague to boys and was teased terribly if they walked too close to me because they were afraid, they'd become my baby's daddy.

Ms. C. did manage to find a couple of tournaments that ended at four o'clock that she signed me up for. I won first or second place in each of those. I was back in decathlon and pulling up the last leg for the team. We won three regional tournaments and one state victory that year. I was ok, I suppose. A little bored, a little lonely.

Studious But Still Stuck

One afternoon while in Dr. Willis' class, he asked me to stay after because he wanted to talk to me and share with me some exciting news. He told me that he sat on the Board at the University of Watson and that they were offering full scholarships for outstanding students like myself. He went on to explain that he had submitted my name as a scholarship recipient.

"Oh, my goodness! Really?"

"Yes Bea, really. You are one of my exceptional students and I was more than happy to recommend you. The Board voted last week and you were one of the three selected across the State of Texas."

"Thank you, Dr. Willis! Thank you so much."

"All I have to do now is meet with your Mom and go over all the details. Once she signs off on it, your college education will be paid for in full. When is a good time to come to your home and speak with her?"

By now I was trembling. I knew for a fact, I had to pre- warn her about all of this. I just stood there trying to come up with something.

"Listen, I tell you what, I will be out of town Monday returning on Wednesday of next week. Let me know if she will be available on that Thursday and I will speak with her then."

"Yes sir, I will let you know."

"Alright then Bea, your senior year should be great with no worries about college."

"Yes, sir and thank you again."

I was so happy; yet, so sad. I just knew she would not let me go to Watson because it was almost two hundred miles away, out of her sight and out of her reach. Once I arrived home, I quickly went through my daily routine. I was trying to gauge what kind of mood she was in before I broke the news to her about the scholarship. She was sitting at the dining room table looking over some papers. I was so scared until I was using the excuse that she was busy not to tell her the news. I had all weekend to tell her, heck, I had until next Thursday. Why bother her now.

"Bea, how was school?"

"It was fine, Mama. Just fine."

"Keep your grades up and Mr. Lee Redford promised me that his law firm would grant you a two-year scholarship to get you started. We will figure out what to do the last two years." *('Lord, help me, now is the time to tell her.')*

"Mama, Dr. Willis, my Black History teacher, told me today that he..." I finished the entire spill, the approval by the Board, the full four-year scholarship, all she had to do is sign, everything.

"You tell that Dr. whoever he is that I said, Hell Naw! You are not going all the way to Watson where it would take two hours to get to you in case something happens. You are going right here in town first. Besides, Watson is almost all negros and that is a bad thing when trying to go to school and learn something. Next thing I know, you would have come up with a baby and have to drop out. So, thanks but no thanks. You be sure and tell him that for me."

"Yes, ma'am."

I knew it. She would rather work four jobs than to not have complete control over me. When I think about how she would not have to work so hard to send me to a four-year university that I could attend on full scholarship, I felt she was being selfish. She was not concerned at all with my education, she was concerned with how she could control my education. The good thing was that Dr. Willis would be back on Wednesday and I would have time to tell him not to show up on Thursday.

When Wednesday rolled around, I noticed Dr. Willis had not returned to class; there was a substitute. He was a man of his word so something unusual must have happened the reason he was absent. A sign of relief came over me because this possibly meant that he would not be back in town on Thursday, either. The entire meeting with Mama would be cancelled and I would have time to explain to him the reason why I wasn't taking the scholarship. The next day, Thursday, Dr. Willis still had not returned. Now, I'm worried. Stopping by Mrs. Ford's office, I inquired if Dr. Willis was alright because he didn't return on Wednesday.

"How sweet of you to ask Bea. He's fine. His flight was overbooked which caused a delay and he had to stay overnight. The next flight out wasn't until today but I am sure he'll be back in class on Friday."

"Thank you, Mrs. Ford. Dr. Willis is one of my favorite teachers."

"And you are one of his favorite students, I assure you that."

I had a pep in my step. Glad that someone felt I was special and the meeting with Mama—cancelled. All was right with my world. Arriving home, I noticed Mama was already there. Maybe she didn't have to go on her second job today. We spoke to each other and I went about my daily routine. Suddenly, there was a knock on the screen door. Mama was sitting at the kitchen table and I was washing dishes, so my hands were wet.

"Go see who's at the door. Never mind your hands are wet. I'll go." When she reached the front door, there stood Dr. Willis. OH MY GOD!! I hurried and dried my hands so that I could rush to his defense. I was sure he was going to need it.

"What do you want?" Mama questioned.

"Mrs. Faye, I'm Bea's Black History teacher and I'd like to congratulate the both of you on Bea receiving a four-year scholarship to the University of Watson."

"What are you congratulating me and Bea for? She's not going!"

"Mrs. Faye, do you mind if I come in and show you the benefits of such a wonderful opportunity for your daughter?"

"Got damn right, I mind! Uppity old ass niggers sitting around trying to figure out how to lure these young girls to that college. Don't nobody give away nothing for free! Ya'll get my baby up there and rape her and take advantage of her because you feel like you can… just because you gave her that school money. I have heard things and she is not going all the way up there to Watson and come back here pregnant, stupid and can't get no job. So, the answer is no thank you!"

"Mrs. Faye, I assure you." Mama started closing the screen door on Dr. Willis.

"I assure you, if you don't get off my porch and out of my face, something bad might happen."

I was standing behind the side of Mama with tears rolling down my face that just wouldn't seem to stop. I was hurt, embarrassed; distraught. Dr. Willis hung his head and left. She slammed and locked the screen door. Once inside, she started chewing me out for not telling Dr. Willis that she had already said no.

"I ought to beat your ass, having some strange man coming up here to my house trying to take you off to who knows where so he can do you some damage."

"I tried to tell him Mama but he was not at school most of the week. He wasn't in class today, either. Mrs. Ford said his flight had been delayed and he would be coming back today. I didn't know he would come straight over here once he was back in town."

"I'm going to call Ford. If I find out you are lying to me, you are going to take off everything and I'm going to whoop you until I feel good!"

Mrs. Ford told Mama everything I told her.

"You better not ever lie to me Gal because I'll find out. Understand?"

I gurgled out a…" Yes, ma'am."

The next day at school was miserable because I had to be in Dr. Willis's class two class periods. One as a Student Assistant and the other as a student. I didn't want to face him. I did not want to go in there and look that man in the face after how Madelene treated him. I just didn't know how much more of this life I could stand. Once inside class, I kept a low profile. I had nothing to say to anyone. When the second class ended, Dr. Willis asked me to stay back a moment. I didn't feel like doing that either but of course I did.

"Listen Bea, I don't want you to dwell on what happened yesterday. Your Mother just loves you too much. She is so afraid of losing you. I can't blame her for that. You are a good kid. She would not make it if something happened to you. You are her world. I'm sorry I couldn't help you with a free ride to Watson but by the time your senior year is over, I'm sure you would have earned some scholarships that will help you here locally. Once again, I am so sorry."

With tears starting to well up in my eyes again, I said, "Me too."

I Can't Take It Anymore

It was Friday, the weekend, and I was really drowning in my sorrows. Madelene was working late and I was home alone. I hated my life so I decided to do something about it. I went in the bathroom medicine cabinet and pulled out a whole bottle of Bayer Aspirin. I started taking handful after handful with a glass of water. I started to feel a little drowsy. I called Dee.

"Dee, I can't take it anymore. Just know that you and Lottie mean the world to me and I pray you both have successful lives. Just promise, you'll remember me ok. Promise?"

"Of course, I'll remember you but where are you going? What are you talking about? Bea? Bea? Oh my God!"

I was awakened by nurses and a doctor trying to make me drink gallons of water. "Drink, drink, if you don't drink, we'll have to pump your stomach." I kept drinking and I kept regurgitating the aspirin into this bucket. They kept checking my vitals and saying,

"You're a lucky girl, we almost lost you. If your friend hadn't found you unconscious and called 911, you might not have been here right now."

"My friend? My friend, Dee. Where is she?"

"She's right outside. Would you like for me to call her?"

"Yes, please."

The nurse left the room and came back with Dee and MADELENE! Oh no, no, no!! After asking a few more questions, the nurse left the room. I begin to speak: "Dee, thank you so much for saving my life, although I no longer want to be here."

"Bea, stop saying that."

Madelene breaks the conversation. "Well, if you didn't want to be here, why didn't you take a bottle of alcohol? Why didn't you spray your mouth full of Raid or rat poison or something like that? I tell you why you didn't because you just want attention—that's all. Now, I've got to try and figure out how to pay this hospital bill because of your pitiful attempt at dying. Dammit to Hell!" She walks out.

This time Dee cries with me. I was released from the hospital and told to rest all weekend and consider seeking wellness counseling. The only thing that would make me well was to be out of the house that Madelene ruled.

I didn't return to school until the Tuesday after Friday's suicide attempt. Everyone was whispering and keeping their distance as if me wanting to kill myself was contagious. I didn't really care what they thought, they didn't know my story.

Everything I tried to do that was right, she would make it out to be wrong. She ruled me with an iron fist; yet, she didn't trust me. She taught me about God but often she didn't listen to Him. I was tired. Obviously, God did not care about my desire to leave this world just yet, so I thank Him that I am still here, sometimes. Time passed and I went back into a shell for a spell. Not really wanting to hang out with my friends or go to the library. I would come home, do my homework, do my chores, take a bath, and go to bed. I didn't even have the desire to watch television or read a book. Now as an adult, I realize I was going through some sort of depression.

Did Mama Trust God Enough?

I knew that I had to get myself together. I had to seek God's face on all of this and roll with the punches. Madelene is who He allowed to adopt me; therefore, I am to learn something from the experiences I had with her. One thing for sure she taught me was how not to treat a child but how to encourage and love him. Another thing I learned is to not pressure someone into doing things out of fear. As a parent, you want the best for your children but you must allow them to make choices. Some of the choices will not be your choices. Some of the choices may turn out to be big mistakes but you must let go so they can grow. You must trust God with them. Perhaps Mama didn't trust God enough with me, she felt He needed her help. Experiencing the emotional, physical, and verbal abuse I went through, let me know she never let Him try; it had to be all her. This parent of mine felt most comfortable being in control of everything. If she could not see it, touch it, twist it, cuss it, beat it, she was a miserable soul.

Somehow, I am more than convinced that came from not being able to trust. Madelene trusted no one. Not family, not friend, not God. Teach me how to trust You, Lord. Teach me.

Chapter Five

It's My Thing, Do What I Wanna Do

Summer before my senior year rolled around. I was finally over feeling sorry for myself and the conditions that made me sorry. Dee introduced me to a guy that was the best friend of her boyfriend, Dell. I always thought it was cute to say: Dee and Dell, all is well?

Mama would not allow me to date or anything, so Steward (Stew for short) and I were introduced at the library. He seemed like a nice guy but I had a picture of my first guy in my head—he didn't look like Stew. Not that Stew was ugly, he was just homely. Dark as midnight, greasy, ashy like he greased himself in Vaseline and missed a few spots. His nose was big and fat but he seemed nice. We talked a lot and met up at the library almost every Saturday.

My First Informed Kiss

One of those Saturdays, Dee had devised a plan to invite the fellows over to her sister's house. Her sister was a grown young woman who worked all day. I didn't understand why we just didn't meet at the library as always. Stew seemed good with the library routine and so did I. Just about every Saturday, Mama would get up and go fishing with Mr. Naylor or by herself; she would stay until at least five o'clock. I would go to the Library around one o'clock and stay until about four. Dee used those same time slots to invite us over. She said she was tired of walking to the library every Saturday and wanted an environment where we could talk out loud and laugh. It sounded innocent so, I agreed to it.

Stew and I met up there and Dee answered the door. Dell was inside sitting on the couch. Stew and I sat in chairs avoiding the small loveseat across from the couch.

"Anybody want a snack? I made some ham sandwiches and there's some chips and dip." I was warned by Mama not to eat at other people's houses because they could put something in your food to make you crazy so you would take your clothes off. But I was hungry. I didn't have lunch because there was only enough chicken and rice left for supper. Mama would be hungry when she came home and I knew there was just enough for the two of us and if

I had eaten my portion for lunch, I would have no supper.

"I think I will have a snack, Dee."

"Go right ahead, everything is on the table." Dee turned the television on Sanford and Son. I fixed my plate and begin to watch.

"Get you something to eat, Stew," Dee suggested.

"Naw, thanks. I'm not hungry."

We watched The Jefferson's and 227 and then things became a little quiet. Awkward was more like it. It had become quiet because Dee and Dell were engulfed in a kiss that brought about moaning and groaning. I was terrified, embarrassed, felt dirty—just totally blown away. They were kissing each other and sticking their tongues down each other's throats like it was their last supper. What was I to do now?

Stew looked at me in a weird way and I begin to tremble with fear. I hopped up and went to the kitchen pretending to refill my plate and my cup with Kool-Aid. Stew, within a blink of an eye, was standing behind me. He gently moved my ponytail to one side of my shoulder and kissed my neck. Lawd! I know where babies come from and this is not where they come from. No, not out of my neck. I need to calm down and breathe. I stood motionless. Stew moved my ponytail to the other side so that he could kiss that side of my neck. Next thing I knew, he had taken my little snack plate out of my hand and sat it on the table. Turning me around, he positioned himself in front of my face. Our eyes met. He moved oh so slowly toward my lips. He placed his lips right on top of mine and parted my lips with his tongue. There it was— my first non-impregnated kiss.

Whatever war of the Kissing Worlds Dell and Dee were going through looked dangerous. I freaked and pulled away from Stew. Unlike the soft kiss on top of my lips from Timmy, Stew lingered inside my mouth. I just knew I had done something that would send me straight to Hell. My reality, according to my upbringing, was if I let a boy kiss me in that way, I would become spoiled for good as a Christian girl.

"I need to go home!" I yelled and stomped out the house.

"Bea, wait, wait! Let me at least walk you back to the library."

"Haven't I let you do enough? Stay away from me! You hear me! Stay away from me!"

I started off running then I slowed to a walk. How could I let this happen to me? I know I said I wanted my first real kiss but I was given the impression by Madelene that I was supposed to be married, engaged and in love when it happened. I didn't love Stew and he didn't love me. We were just sixteen years old. It felt nice for someone to kiss me but at the same time it felt wrong.

I suppose Dee was embarrassed about the way I behaved that day but I didn't care. I knew I couldn't conceive from a kiss but somehow, I had to protect myself from Madelene and the only way to do that was to do what she said. Even when she wasn't watching or was she?

My Senior Year

Time flew by. It was the beginning of my senior year. I received a two-year scholarship to Seawall Southwest Junior College with hopes of moving away from Mama the last two years. My brief stent on the drill team made me think about dance as a Minor. Besides, after looking over their curriculum, there weren't many electives available. The schedule showed one speech class and one Jazz Dance class. I purposed to sign up for speech in the Fall and Jazz Dance in the Spring semesters.

Seniors were happy and afraid all at the same time and they wanted answers. What would life after high school bring? Would they make it in college? Would there be enough money or would they have to drop out? These questions often came up in my mind. I decided to approach Mama with one of my questions after supper.

"Mama, do you think I will make it through all four years of college?"

"You sure as in hell better! I have not been wiping babies' assess and cleaning folks houses for nothing! You are going to college and you are going to get a teaching degree and make something of yourself!"

"Yes, ma'am."

I just didn't have the strength to argue, excuse me, discuss the teacher major anymore. Why couldn't she see that I didn't want to be a teacher? I'm not good with kids. The first babysitting job I had was with two neighborhood boys. They were alright but they ran me ragged…chasing them, feeding them, cleaning them up. At this point, I was certain that I didn't want any kids in my house and I sure didn't want to teach them. *('Dear Lord, Let there be a way that I can graduate with a degree in Business with an emphasis in Marketing and live to tell about it.')*

It Wasn't All Bad

Several nice things happened in my senior year. I was voted Vice President of the Student Council and President of the Speech Club. I was recommended for Student of the Year (which I did not win) and was chosen to grace the cover of the local community newspaper. There was a photo of me doing my dramatic interpretation of Joan of Arc. Ms. C. chose me to represent the Department in a community spotlight and I was so excited.

Things at home were different from the previous year. I am not sure what happened to Mr. Naylor but suddenly Mama was dating a deacon that didn't belong to our church! Not knowing all the details, I was thrown into an introduction one day when I came home from school.

"Bea, I want you to meet Deacon Stanford. He's a Deacon over at True Way Baptist Church."

"Pleased to meet you, sir." (The nerve of this woman dating a man whose last name sounds like my Papa's first name! Sanford/Stanford… humph!)

"Pleased to meet you as well, Bea. Your Mother has told me so many wonderful things about you." (SAY WHAT?? Then why doesn't she ever tell me???)

"Bea, I understand that you are a senior in high school this year."

"Yes, sir."

"So, what are your plans after graduation?" (This told me that I still wasn't the main topic of any of Madelene's conversations.)

"Junior college, then on to a four-year university."

"Do you have in mind which four-year you would like to attend?" Ok, if this is small talk with this man, I am done. I don't feel like answering any more questions. None of your business! That's what I wanted to blurt out. Madelene takes over the conversation with her famous controlling interruptions.

"Bea is going to Liberty State when she's done at Southwest. She's going to be a teacher, you know." Grrr! I hate it when she does that. No decisions can be made by me and me alone. She must have total control in my life no matter what.

"That's a good school, Bea. I graduated from there myself with a degree in Business." If I were a rabbit, my ears would have been standing straight up.

"Business?"

"Yes, my Bachelor's degree is in Business. My Master's degree is in Finance. I am glad you chose Liberty."

"Thank you."

I didn't choose Liberty. I chose Watson. Liberty was only forty-five minutes away and that was not far enough away for me. I knew the only reason she wanted me to go to Liberty was so she could make a forty-five minute run to spy on me and find a reason to beat me half to death if she even thought I was doing anything wrong and make me come back home. I was determined that would not happen.

"Oh, ok. Well, if you will excuse me, I have chores to do and homework to complete, nice meeting you."

As I walked off, I heard him say, "She is such a nice young lady."

"Why thank you, Deacon Stanford. I haven't had a moments trouble out of Bea." (Yeah, that's because I don't want to die!)

"She's a good girl." (If he only knew. I really don't think I would have been a "bad" girl by choice but I guess I should be thankful that I was never given such a choice.)

There were evenings when they would go to dinner and come to the house and talk a long time. I really wasn't too fond of those evenings because I had to stay out of the living room area where the "grown folks" were.

I Had A Right to Prom

Dee called me on the rotary phone and I quickly took it into my bedroom. "Bea, are you going to prom?"

"Prom?" I hadn't really thought about prom because I was almost certain that when I ask Madelene if I could go, the answer to that would be a "NO".

"I hadn't really thought about it, Dee. I probably won't go."

"But you have to go! You are a senior and the prom is our rite of passage!" This girl was overly dramatic and she always made things seem more important than they were.

"Well, I guess I lost my rights then!"

"No, Bea. You have to go."

"I have to go. And why is that Dee?" I could feel that she had made up some sort of plan, just like she did that day at her sister's house.

"Uh, well, Dell's cousin was stationed here at the Army base about a month ago and Dell invited him to our prom."

"What? Why would an Army guy want to go to a high school prom? He's a man?"

"Actually, he is only 18. He finished high school a little early and went right into the Army. So, you see, he may be a soldier but he is a young soldier. Dell and I are already 18 and you will be 18 the month after we graduate, so you see he is our equal."

"What does all of this have to do with me, Dee?"

"He needs a date, Bea."

"Dell invited him, let one of Dell's sisters find him a date."

"Bea, now you know that Dell's sisters' friends are wild and always in the streets. This guy is nice and well- mannered. His father is a preacher and Dell says he graduated from high school with honors just like you are about to do."

"So, you think that Madelene is going to let me go to a prom with a guy in the Army that she doesn't know? You have got to be out of your mind!

"What if my Mom tells her that she doesn't want me to go alone with Dell and it would be best if we double dated."

"I don't know Dee. I don't know if it would be worth the trouble."

"Come on Bea, it's senior prom."

"Why do I have a feeling that I'm going to regret this?"

"You won't regret it. I promise."

"Okay, I guess if you can get your Mom to convince her, I'll go."

"You're the best Bea, talk to you later."

What have I done? I know better. One thing Madelene didn't like was sneaky schemes. And besides, what would I wear? I don't have anything formal in my closet. Oh my God, this is such a mistake, I'm calling Dee back. But before I could call Dee back, the phone rang and it was for Mama. It was Dee's mother, Ms. Mae, on the phone. Dang, that girl works fast. Knowing her, she had already mapped all of this out with her mother before she called me. I noticed that Madelene was listening attentively to Mae and not saying much. This meant that Mae was shifting into high gear to make this prom double date thing happen. I could not imagine what the result might be. It really didn't matter to me either way. I eased dropped on the conversation.

"I don't know about all of this, Mae. I just don't think that good Christian girls should be going anywhere with no boys late at night."

"I understand your reasoning Madelene. That's why I suggested they go together. I never had the chance to go to a prom or finish high school because my Mama was sick my last year of school. I stayed home to take care of her. I finally earned my GED but I missed all the wonderful things that seniors in high school get the chance to experience. I just don't want that for Dee and I know you don't want it for Bea, either. Do you?" (Dee's mama was good!)

"Since you put it that way, I suppose you could be right. I only finished the fourth grade, so I don't know much about school, college, or any of those things that education has to offer. That is why I keep a tight rein on Bea. I do not want her to be a hoe like her real Mama—get stuck with a baby and there goes her future." Not realizing that statement might have been a bit offensive to Ms. Mae since she got "stuck" with a baby at an early age, Ms. Mae interrupted Mama and said, "So it's settled, the girls will double date on prom night."

"Yea, I guess so. But I don't want Bea coming in this house after midnight. Don't no good Christian girl stay out all hours of the night with no boy. That's the devil's time to prowl and cause things to happen."

"Wait a minute, Madelene. Dee is not exactly a street walker or anything. She's a good Christian girl, too. Just because I want her to have a complete high school experience, it doesn't mean she is going to do something bad because the clock strikes twelve."

"Not past midnight or she doesn't go. That's final." She hung up on Ms. Mae. As I pulled my head back from around the corner, I didn't know whether to be happy or afraid. I was going to the prom, with a boy—no, a soldier. Hot Damn!

"Bea, get your ass in here." I had to pretend that I knew nothing of her previous conversation.

"Now, I know you and Dee made up this little scheme to go to this prom. I agreed to let you go."

"Oh, thank you, Mama."

I ran toward her to give her a hug and she held her big lumberjack arm out that stopped me dead in my tracks.

"Don't try to hug up to me because there are conditions. You must be back in this house by twelve midnight or else I'm coming after you." Now, I knew that the prom ended at twelve so was she not allowing drive time back to the house. If she wasn't that meant that we had to leave the prom at eleven thirty. If this had been discussed with Dee's mom, then I am sure everything will be fine.

"Yes, ma'am, Mama, thank you."

"You are welcome. You make good grades and all, so I suppose I have taught you how to keep your legs closed and be a lady."

"Oh, but Mama, what am I going to wear?"

"Got dammit to hell! I forgot about that. We'll go to the Goodwill Store tomorrow and see what we can find."

I was so excited. Most of my clothes came from Goodwill anyway but by the time they were washed and ironed then hung up, they looked brand new. I was so excited. I was going to the prom and with a soldier!

The Perfect Dress

The next day couldn't come fast enough. When school was out, Mama picked me up and we headed to Goodwill. Turns out we weren't the only mother and daughter team from the neighborhood looking for prom dresses. Sis. Charlotte and her daughter, Candace, from the church were in there. They pretended not to see us and tried to hurry and leave the store. Mama stopped them dead in their tracks.

"Hey Charlotte, you find anything in here worth wearing to a prom?"

"Uh, uh, oh…Hi, Madelene and Bea." Candace tried to hide behind her mom as if you couldn't see her. She was about a Size 20 and her mama a Size 8!

"We found a dress for my niece. They really didn't have anything Candace could wear. Good luck, hope you find something."

She scurried over to the check out. I caught a glimpse of the dress she purchased for her "niece" on the counter. I took a photocopy of it in my head because that dress would be what Candace wore to the prom. Ms. Charlotte must have forgotten that everyone in town knew she was the best seamstress this side of Heaven. She could take a potato sack and make a coat. So, even if wasn't the right size, Sis. Charlotte could make it work.

"You see how that heifer lied. She knows good and damn well that she is going to make that dress fit her baby cow. That's what I can't stand about some folks…Always pretending that they are somebody big, special, have money and all that stuff when they know that they are just as poor as the next person. I'm proud of my poor and I am not going to lie about it and I'm grateful for what I have. Don't you be like that Bea…all uppity and sh_ just because you think you have a few dollars. Not even when you graduate from college and start teaching school, you hear me?" (Oh Lord, here we go with this teaching stuff again. I do NOT want to be a teacher. Read my thoughts Mama; read my thoughts!)

"Yes, ma'am."

We went from rack to rack but found nothing that was pretty or stylish. Not finding anything started me to feeling a little down.

"Let's go, I have another store I go to sometimes because they have good sales."

This store was a secondhand boutique store. Designer clothes were on consignment from rich folks that didn't want them anymore. Mrs. Core was the other lady Mama worked for twice a week and she never bought anything new accept groceries. She must have told Mama about this place. I was in awe. Everything in the store smelled new. It was just like going into JC Penny's or Sears. The sales lady in the store knew Mama by name. This could only mean that Mama came in here a lot with or without Mrs. Core.

"Hello, Kippy. What can I do for you today?" Kippy is what Mrs. Core called Mama because her ninety-year-old father called her that. So that became her nickname around their household.

"I'm looking for a prom dress for my daughter. She's a senior this year and she's going to college to become a teacher."

"That is so nice. She certainly is a beautiful girl." (How could that be. Mama said I wasn't pretty; that I was her little flat nosed baby and nobody would ever love me or think I was pretty except her.)

"Let's take a look over here on our sales rack."

The clothes on the sales rack were pricy so I wondered what the prices were for the items not on sale. Madeline looked through the dresses and didn't see anything she liked. The sales lady saw the disappointment in her face and went to a room in the back of the store.

"I don't see anything Bea. What do you think?" (WHAT?? She asked my opinion!)

"I don't really see anything that I like yet." "Do you see anything?"

"Naw, not really." Just then, the sales lady brought this beautiful floral teal and pink dress from the back.

"What do you think about this one, Kippy?"

"Oh, that's real pretty. Can she go and try it on?"

"Of course, come this way." The dress fit perfectly. I felt like Cinderella. I didn't want to think about turning back into rags at midnight at all. When I walked out, both Madelene and the sales lady's eyes lit up.

"You look beautiful, Bea." The sales lady's compliment made me feel so special. Madelene's only words were "How much?"

"Kippy, we'll talk about that in a moment."

"No, I want to talk about it right now. It's pretty and all but if I can't afford it then all this is for nothing."

"Bea, would you mind going back in the dressing room to change?" the sales lady asked.

"Oh no, ma'am."

I didn't know what was going on. I just hoped with all my heart that Mama could afford this dress. The bell of the ball I would become in this dress. After changing, I came back out as the sales lady went back in to retrieve the dress. She brought it out in a plastic bag with a receipt attached to it that said Paid in Full, $100.00.

Oh, my goodness, one hundred dollars. How on earth did she pay for that? I dare not ask. On the way home, Mama was quiet. I looked at her and it looked as if she had been crying or wanted to cry. So badly I wanted to ask what was wrong but was afraid to. Once in the house she spoke.

"No matter what Bea, always keep God first in your life. He will make a way out of no way. He will provide your every need and some of your wants. Promise me Bea, you'll always make Him first."

"I promise."

It turns out that inspirational message was inspired by Mrs. Core. The sales lady knew that Mama couldn't afford that dress so she called Mrs. Core and she told her to give it to Mama and she would pay for it as my graduation present. I suppose the brief softness I saw in her that day was called 'Grateful to God'. And so was I.

Cinderella Never After

It was the week before the prom and Mama had required that my escort to come over so she could lay eyes on him. His name was Edward. We had talked on the telephone everyday trying to get to know each other. He was taller than me, slim yet, muscular. He spoke respectfully soft and extended his hand out to Mama when he met her.

"Have a seat." He sat down on the couch while she sat in her high back gold chair and I sat on the love seat straight across from her. This was so she could see my facial expressions depending on what she would ask him. Much to my surprise, she did not give him the Madelene drill. She told him that she respected the Armed Forces. Then, she told him that he would respect her daughter or else he might come up missing when it was time to go back. I watched beads of sweat pop up on Edward's head.

"Oh, no problem ma'am. No problem at all."

"And you better have her back here at midnight. You understand me?"

"Yes, ma'am. Understood."

"Alright, you can leave now." I didn't, for the first time, worry about what type of impression Madelene made on Edward. I just wanted to dress up and go on a date. Maybe it was a date, maybe not.

When Edward left, she told me that she could see in his eyes that he was sneaky and not to let him kiss or rub on me because she didn't want to shoot both of us. Fear did not cover me this time. I was almost grown and besides, I didn't like Edward like that, yet.

Saturday was here. It was early in the morning, I couldn't sleep any longer. Jumping out of bed, I dressed, washed up and started doing my regular Saturday chores. Madelene was sitting on the porch smoking a cigarette; I hated those things. They always made me cough.

"Bea?" Skipping to the front door stopping right in front of the screen, I answered, "Yes, ma'am?"

"You know, I've been thinking about changing my mind about this whole prom thing. I just don't like the way that boy looks on the inside. Something about him is not sitting well in my spirit. Nope, you're not going."

"No, not going? But Mama the tickets are already bought, the dress is already bought, and Miss Mable pressed my hair yesterday. You spent money Mama and now you are not going to let me go?"

"Mrs. Core paid for that dress. Miss Mable owed me a favor and I have five dollars to pay the boy back for the ticket. I've made up my mind. You are staying your ass at home. What was I thinking? Throwing you out there in a pack of wolves?"

She flicked the ashes off her cigarette and kept on smoking, mumbling to herself. I was devastated I could barely move. Before leaving the door, I tried one more plea.

"Mama, this might mean Dee can't go at all if I don't go with her. That would spoil her senior prom. Don't you think?"

"Nice try but I know Mae. She was going to let her girl go anyway. She and Dee cooked this scheme up just so you could go. I'm not stupid. I really thought about letting you go until I met this

Edward character. I don't think he's safe. I've already called Mae and she understands. Dee is going to take lots of pictures. So, go on now, finish your chores. We have peaches to pick after a while."

That day was the day that I was reminded how much I hated my life. Trapped, no way out. I hated picking peaches. I hated being afraid of her all the time. I hated living. That evening, I laid across my bed and cried myself to sleep.

The following Monday, Dee couldn't wait to show me all the photos of the prom. It looked as if she had such a good time. Dell was so handsome in his royal blue tux and Dee looked like she had won the Miss Black America Pageant in her royal blue and silver gown. Tears starting streaming down my face after about the third photo. Dee gave me a hug and said how sorry she was that I didn't get to go after all. Edward was disappointed, too. I asked her did he go after all and she said he did but that he mainly sat at the table. Every now and then, he would walk over and ask a girl that didn't have a date to dance. Then, he would come back and sit down. Dee showed me a picture of him in his uniform that he wore that night. All the girls that showed up stag begged him to take a picture with them. I would have been the envy of all those girls. Another mass production of destruction orchestrated by Madelene Faye. What else is new?

Graduation Day

Graduation was a week away now. I asked Madelene did she let Papa know when the ceremony was and she said yes. That made me smile. I would finally get to see him. Madelene invited Dec. Stanford to the graduation, too. I'm not sure if she did that to make Papa jealous or just to show other women that she could get a decent Christian man. If that was the case, I am sure they all asked, "How?"

I rode to the ceremony with Dee because we all had to arrive early for rehearsal. Feeling accomplished, I was happy that day. It was a feeling of joy, excitement and nervousness. As we marched in, I spotted Papa! The urge to run out of line and embrace him was overwhelming but I kept marching. Having the last name Faye was an advantage because it wasn't long before they called my name. "Bea Coral Faye." I stepped proudly on the stage with an honor cord and three medals. Out of four hundred students, I was ranked number six. I paused for a photo as the Superintendent handed me my High School Diploma. I had made it through high school despite the emotional and physical scars received at the hands of an abusive mother. So grateful was I.

After the ceremony, Papa waited for me. I ran to him and held on to him for dear life.

"I miss you so much Papa."

"I know, I miss you too. Don't ever think I don't love you just because Maddy chose to divorce me. Nothing will ever change that.

You will always be my baby girl." I cried. Madelene shows up in the middle of our reunion with the deacon.

"Hello, Sanford."

"Madeline."

"This is Deacon (placing the emphasis on deacon as if to indicate that she had stepped up a grade from him) Stanford."

"Hey, man, pleased to meet you."

"Likewise."

"Come on Bea. We should get going if we are going to beat the line at Sirloin Stockade."

"Bye, Papa." With one last hug, I walked away trying to hold back the tears. I would have given anything to have him come along with us. There was no way a thought like that ran across her mind.

The line at Sirloin Stockade was long but it moved quickly. Not feeling hungry, I picked at my food. Madelene gave me the evil eye as if to say I better eat all my food because Dec. was paying for it and you could not take a doggy bag. As a high school graduate and an almost 18-year-old, I decided to approach my appetite like an adult.

"Deacon Stanford, I want to apologize if I don't eat everything on my plate. Today is such a big day for me and I am just too excited to eat."

"Oh, don't you worry about that Bea. Eat what you can and have no concern about what is left on your plate."

"Thank you, sir." "Madelene squinted her eyes and lowered her head as she continued eating. For once, she had nothing to say.

After Graduation

It was summer once again. My counselor prior to graduation recommended me for a summer position at the YWCA. It was a resident advisor position and it required that I stay overnight twice a week. In the daytime, I worked at a retail store, Craigs Men's Wear in the mall, dressing mannequins for the store windows. I dressed the mannequins inside the store, too. The summer income allowed me to buy clothes for college and place some in a savings account I was saving for my transition to Liberty.

One Saturday afternoon while working at Craigs, Edward walks in the store in uniform, no less. I tried to avoid him but he spotted me and approached me head on.

"Bea, how have you been?" He had such a pretty smile, especially since he wasn't sweating bullets from Madelene.

"Fine. How about yourself?"

"I'm good. Are you purchasing something for someone?"

"No, I work here. Would you like for me to direct you to a salesman for some assistance?"

"No, I am a regular at this store but I've never seen you in here before."

"I just started working here after graduation."

"If you don't mind me asking, what is it that you do?"

"I am what you call a display designer."

"Oh, so you dress the mannequins?"

"Yes, I dress the mannequins." We both laughed.

"Don't let me interrupt your shopping; good seeing you again."

"Same here."

Thinking about how Madelene treated him made me feel a little embarrassed. I suppose that's why I tried to avoid him at first. I wish I'd had the opportunity to get to know him better. He really seemed like a nice guy. I went about my assignment in the storeroom sorting out shirts and ties to dress this one mannequin when I felt a tap on my shoulder. It was the Assistant Manager.

" Bea, Soldier Boy wants to speak to you", she said with a sheepish grin.

"Soldier Boy?" I walked out of the storeroom and there stood Edward. I thought he had left the store already.

"Oh, Edward, is there something I can help you with?"

"As a matter of Fact, there is. If you haven't had your lunch break yet, I'd like to take you to lunch."

"I don't actually have a lunch break, only fifteen-minute breaks. But thanks for asking."

"How about dinner, then?"

"Dinner? I work at night, as well, so I would have to work dinner out."

"That's fine. May I have your number so I can call and see if you worked things out?" Thinking quickly because Madelene would not take too kindly to this guy calling her house, especially after she said he was sneaky.

"Listen, let me give you a call from my night job when I have it figured out."

"Fair enough." He wrote his number on one of the ads that lay on the counter and handed it to me.

"Here you go."

"Thanks Edward. You'll hear from me soon." Of course, I lied. I had no intention of calling him at all, although he had piqued my interest in a different way than before. One night about three weeks later, Dee called me at the Y.

"Hey girl, long time no see."

"Yeah, I know. Just working night and day."

"Dell and I were riding around and we just happened to stop right outside the Y."

"You are outside?"

"Yep."

"Let me secure everything and I'll be right out. I can't be outside long but I want to see you."

"Ok, we'll be here."

I must admit I missed Dee as I thought about how Lottie abandoned us for some guy she met in the Air Force. She married right out of high school because she was pregnant and didn't want anyone to know because they were strong Pentecostals. We would have loved her anyway but her mother made her marry and they moved away somewhere. But Dee, she was always there for me. She was in a dental assistance program at the Medical Institute campus.

I locked the doors to the office and to the hallway where the girls resided and hurried outside to the front steps of the building. I pushed the door open and laid eyes on Dee, Dell, and Edward. Edward!! What was he doing here with them? Oh, that's right he and Dell are cousins but did they have to bring him along? I didn't want him to know where my night job was. He could sneak around here and rape me or something. Wait a minute. STOP! Bea, you are sounding like Madelene. Pump the breaks, calm down and act civil.

"Hey guys. Glad to see all of you. And Edward, what a surprise."

"Yeah Bea, Dell and I asked Edward to come along since you never contacted him after he saw you in Craigs that day," she said raising one eyebrow.

"Oh, I am sure Edward understands how busy I am. Why just look at the fact that my best friend had to come and visit me on one of my jobs. It was not intentional that that communication didn't happen."

We all sat down on the steps during my short thirty-minute break making small talk. It was time for me to go back inside.

"Time to go back to work. Thank all of you for stopping by. I promise, I will try and stay in contact a little better than I have been." I tried to rush up the steps and get back inside before Edward said anything. I was not quick enough.

"Bea, I know you are busy. I can see that for myself now but do you mind if I call sometime?" Now, I knew there was no way Edward could call my house and I not be punished for it. How was he going to call me?

"Do you still have my number?" Truth was, I had no idea what I did with his phone number so there was a pause.

"Look, here it is again and I would REALLY like to talk to you sometime, if that's ok?"

"Sure, I will give you a call."

"Promise?"

"I promise."

I watched him walk off. He was not bad, not bad at all. I didn't know how to handle his interest. Was his interest in me as a person or what was in between my legs like Madelene has always said was a man's motive? I would have to give this some thought before I ever dialed his number, deep thought.

It was two weeks later around nine-thirty at night. All the resident girls were gone on a retreat and I was there alone in the building, bored out of my mind. I had read all of Proverbs, then, I finished *How Stella God Her Groove* back by Terry McMillan and started skimming through the newspaper and simply ran out of things to read. I had to remain at the front desk until midnight, so by now I was just twiddling my thumbs. I thought perhaps I would organize the desk drawer, again. When I opened the drawer, there was Edward's telephone number. Surprised that the day staff hadn't thrown it away, I sat staring at it. Madelene was in my head: Nice Christian girls don't call boys. Nice Christian girls are not out late at night with boys. All you do is give them the idea that they can do what they want with you.

I decided that since I was eighteen years old and Edward was almost nineteen, I was a young woman and he was a young man, and I could call him if I wanted too! So, I did. We had a nice long talk. We talked a long time and laughed a lot. Before I knew it, it was past midnight and time for me to go upstairs for the night. I thought about trying to spend some time with Edward but how could I? I worked both day and night and I would be going to college in September. It was the end of July and I had a goal and a mission. Maybe another conversation one of these evenings, maybe not.

I Suspect

The next Monday when I clocked in at Craigs and started my assignments for the day, the Assistant Manager came to the back and said there was something at the front desk for me. I gathered the ensembles together that I wanted to switch out and headed toward the front desk. My eyes enlarged when I saw a beautiful vase with two dozen roses inside and a small card attached. The card said, 'Meet me in the food court after your shift, please. Edward.'

I smiled and took the flowers to the back. I couldn't make up my mind whether to go to the food court or not, so I just kept working. One of the girls who worked the shift after me called in sick. I volunteered to take her shift since I didn't have to work at the Y that night. I called Madelene and told her I picked up a second shift. I was saved from meeting Edward. I was afraid anyway. One of the saddest things to happen to an individual is to be afraid of yourself. So many negative things had been programmed into my brain by Madelene until I was afraid to trust myself. Fear of oneself is a crazy fear. But I didn't ask for it, I acquired it. There had to be a way that I could reprogram that spirit of fear that she embedded inside me at such an early age. At some point, I had to start believing in myself, trusting myself and most of all, learning how to love myself—the hardest task of all.

I made up my mind that I would start the reprogramming tonight by giving Edward a call to thank him for the beautiful flowers. Also, I wanted to apologize for not meeting him in the food court but I had taken a second shift. I went to the employee lounge in the back of the store and gave him a call.

He was disappointed that I didn't meet him for lunch but asked if I could meet him during my next break. On the evening shift, you were allowed thirty minutes, so I said yes. We met in front of the store and walked down to a bench in front of the ice cream shop.

"I really like you, Bea. I wanted to meet with you to let you know I am being stationed in West Virginia, so I only have two weeks left here in Texas."

"Wow, that has to be exciting—having a chance to travel and all."

"It's just all part of being in the military. I don't know when or if I will get back to Texas but I want us to keep in touch."

"Oh, you know Dee and Dell will see to that." We both laughed.

I was thinking that if I was going to break out of fear, I needed to do it in a big way. I invited Edward to the Y the next night that I would be working. He agreed to show up around eleven. I let him in and we really enjoyed ourselves talking and laughing about everything that had gone on in our lives. Even some of the bad things. The girls were on another retreat. I was alone and it was after one o'clock in the morning. I didn't want Edward to leave so I invited him up to my room. He sat in the spare chair that rested in the corner of my drab, barely furnished room. I wanted to lie down. I invited him to lie down with me. What happened between us next sent my mind into a whirlwind. Seeing him again after that night might not be an option. But I was so thankful to have experienced the feeling of intimate love, even if it wasn't real.

I had fallen asleep with the phone in my hand. I never made the call.

Chapter Six
THE FIRST TWO YEARS

With summer over and Fall Semester starting at SJC, I really began to feel grown up and independent.

Madelene was in a full swing romance with Deacon Stanford and trying to make the impression on him that she was a sweet woman. She pretended to be so sweet around him until he nicknamed her Bunny. I often wondered why that name.

So Basically, Basic

Nevertheless, Junior College was alright. It's just that to me, it was so easy and uneventful. Most of my classes were on Mondays, Wednesdays and Fridays with my elective classes being held on Tuesdays and Thursdays. The College was rather small so there were not a lot of classes to choose from. I took most of my basic classes so that when I moved on to Liberty, I could solely concentrate on my major, Business. The Student Union Building was the neatest hangout. Students were meeting and greeting, talking, and laughing. It was a whole new world for me. It was apparent that I hadn't been around large groups of people outside of church before. When I was on campus, I pretended that I was living in a dorm that was far away from Madelene. I would stay there until I graduated with two degrees and then, I would go out into the world and be a grand success. It was just a thought. I could have done that if she would have signed for the scholarship Dr. Willis wanted to award me. Well, no use crying over spilled milk. I'm here. I am still at home and every step I take, I feel the pressure of her rules and the stinging of her hand. The two electives I chose were Jazz Dance and Speech.

My New Escape

The tournament experience I had in high school made me a real standout in the Speech class. It was fun. But my dance class, now that was a challenge. Mama didn't allow me to dance, so I was awfully bad at it, at first. I happened to be paired with a partner, Josiah, who was a year ahead of me. We both graduated from the same high school where he was a standout football player. I felt as if he must have taken dance for the reason I did: lack of electives. We were to practice basic jazz moves in class and for our final, we were to choreograph our own piece. Josiah (Josh) was quite good at Jazz Dance and the fact that he looked like a bronze Greek God didn't hurt either. In those days, I was a tiny Size 8 so Josh was able to pick me up and toss me around like a penny. Jazz Dance became another escape. It was an escape that I very much needed because when Madelene was angry with Deacon, she would take it out on me. Yelling and fussing about everything. As the situation with him became resolved, she'd ease up on me; seems as if I was her emotional punching bag.

That first year in junior college flew by. I was already in my last semester before moving on to Liberty. The bright side of the continued education trek was that I would be out of the house and on my own! It was amazing how far I had come in Jazz Dance with Josh's help. We did a great job on our final and Ms. Masters, our instructor, wanted to showcase us at the end of the year's dance recital. Neither of us would eat lunch, we'd head to the Dance Gym to practice every day. Together, we choreographed to *The Look of Love* by Isaac Hayes.

Here We Go Again

An invitation was mailed to all parents. I never expected Madelene to show up but she did, along with Deacon Stanford. She never came to any of my speeches, performances…nothing. Why she chose to come to this dance recital, I don't know. There were several groups before it was our turn. I could not lose focus just because Madelene was in the audience. I knew I was good at this and for once, I didn't care what she thought. The dance was sensual, graceful and powerful. We received three standing ovations that night. As we kept running back out to take our bows, I couldn't help but notice that everyone was sanding except for Madelene. Even Deacon Stanford was standing and consistently clapping his hands. Ms. Masters awarded us with advanced medals and chose us as the Best Performers at the recital. Josh and I were so excited. We ran backstage and impulsively gave each other a hug. When the embrace was released, there stood Madelene ready to grab and put her hands on me but Ms. Masters appeared.

"Oh, you must be Bea's Mom? I am so glad to finally meet you."

She ushered Madelene from backstage so that we could change and go celebrate—for me, so I could go home. Ms. Masters saved me the embarrassment in front of Josh and the other dancers. I was extremely grateful for that. Once at home, I had to sit in the living room while she sat in the high back velvet gold chair and I on the judgement seat— the green ottoman.

"I was never so ashamed before in my life, you and that boy carrying on like you were in bed together! I wanted to come up there and jerk you off that stage. And Deacon Stanford had to watch that hoe stuff come out of you in front of him and God and everybody. I am so mad! Hurt! ashamed! I didn't realize that the Deacon was there in the kitchen.

He emerges and says, "Now Bunny, you stop being so hard on Bea. It was a beautiful dance and I know that her teacher thought it was really great."

"I don't give a heck what her teacher thought. She should not allow such outrageous movement to happen between a boy and a girl like that!"

"Well, would you rather Bea dance with a girl like that?" (Whoa, you go Deacon.)

"I think it is time for you to leave."

"Alright, I will call you tomorrow. Bea, you did an excellent job tonight. I know I'm not your father but I was so proud." As he made that last statement, he walked out the door. Maybe ole Deke wasn't so bad after all.

"I am going to have to get rid of him. No man is going to come in my house and try and make me look bad in front of my own child. I run you; you don't run you, and nobody else. I am letting him know that unless he can stay out of my business with you, he and I are through." Madelene was really upset that he defended me until I never received part two of the hoe-like-your-mama lecture.

"You go wash that nastiness off your body and get in the bed. I will be glad when you leave that school. And you are not allowed to take anymore dance classes, you understand me?"

"Yes, ma'am." It is just as well at Liberty there were plenty other electives I could choose from. Another ending to a Madelene kill my joy chapter. But you know, it really didn't bother me that bad. Perhaps it was because in less than two months, I would be moving into a dorm room on the Liberty campus. Although it was not my choice to attend there, at this phase of my escape plan, I'll take it. For the next couple of months, I kept the job at the Y. It paid the most money and besides, it allowed me to stay overnight on Friday and Saturday nights away from you know who.

She Ain't All Bad

I must admit, Madelene did something nice for me. She negotiated with the lawyer she worked for and came up with a car for me to drive back and forth to the University. I remember when she tried to teach me how to drive. It was a nightmare! She hit me all upside my head when I would make a mistake. Finally, she decided she would find a way to send me to Driver's Education School and let them teach me. I was so glad she did. I passed the written test but had problems with the driver's portion because I didn't know how to back in between those cones without knocking them down. Still don't! I am a horrible backer until this day. None the less, the car she bought was a Honda Civic. The tiny tin can ones they made when they first came out. Once that car was in the driveway, I practiced backing up a lot. On a Saturday morning, I went to retake the driver's portion of the test and because the car was so tiny, I whipped right in between those cones and passed. It was so much nicer to drive myself to work instead of waiting on her to take me or to pick me up.

Twenty was approaching me and I kept thinking back on some things. Like the time I applied for a job with Brandis Airlines last summer and never heard from them; especially after they told me how impressed they were with my qualifying scores. I couldn't figure it out. Training would be in Dallas and once I earned my wings, I'd fly all over the world. I wanted that freedom so bad. Here it was a summer later, almost time to leave and move away when I found it. There was a letter under a pile of other mail on the dining table; the letter was from Brandis Airline. It stated that I had been chosen for the Hostess Airline Training Program but since I did not respond to the offer, the slot was given to someone else and they were apologetic. Tears rolled down my face. She had kept that information from me.

Why? Why did she insist on making my life miserable? I had followed all her rules, why didn't she notice that? Why couldn't she let me go? She hadn't arrived home from work yet. I took the letter and hid it in my Bible that I took with me everywhere. I never spoke a word to her that I knew what she had done— that she had once again ruined an opportunity for me to be independent and successful. I resented her method of parenting so badly. I was hurt and I was angry. I was kept from everything. I stayed away from everything and everybody she told me to stay away from. I kept high standards so that she would not be embarrassed and all I wanted was the opportunity to live my life. Another piece of me died that day. It hit me hard in the chest that she didn't love me. She just needed to control me.

After that day, I made up in my mind that I was going to experience some things, conquer some things and live my life quietly all around her without her knowing it. Yes, I was thinking a lot that day. I needed to make that dream I had a reality.

It's My Life

One night, Edward gives me a call at the Y. We chatted a bit as he told me he just wanted to say goodbye. He was being stationed in West Virginia. He asked me if I wanted to spend my break with him, since he was going away. Not thinking, I told him I had all night because the girls were on a retreat.

"Oh really, so you are not dorm sitting tonight, huh?"

"No, but I can't leave the property."

"Bea, I knew that before I called you. Wishful thinking is that you let me inside to keep you company while we talk the night away. What do you say?" We could have visitors but only until midnight when it was time to lock up and go to bed. It was almost eleven and I thought that an hour of conversation with this young man couldn't hurt.

"Alright Soldier, your wish has come true. I will let you in only until midnight, then it's lights out."

"Good enough."

"How long will it take you to get here?"

"Actually, I'm around the corner at the Seven-Eleven talking to you on the pay phone." I was slightly impressed that he would stand on a pay phone for over forty-five minutes just to talk to me. *(All men are dogs; they just want to get in your drawers. Nobody is ever going to love you except me, nothing is for free: Madelene's subliminal messages.)* Ignoring the messages, I told Edward to come on over and I would let him in. As he approached the front door, my hands started to shake wondering if I had done the right thing. This was a lot scarier than my dream. *(Another Madelene brain wave: he could rape you or something.)* Too late to retreat, there he is on the other side of the door, looking more attractive than I remember.

"Come on in."

"Thanks Bea." He leaned in and gave me a hug. There was a wait bench right across from the front desk. We sat there making small talk. The tone of the conversation switched.

"Bea, I really like you. I have liked you since the beginning when Dee told me what a wonderful Christian girl you were. I was raised in an extremely strict religious family, as well. I was adopted by my Aunt and Uncle when I was just a baby. My real Mother died at a young age from a mysterious gunshot wound. They have not found the shooter after all these years."

"Wow, I was adopted, too but by my biological Mother's great aunt. So are your Aunt and Uncle still living?"

"No, Aunt Miracle was found shot to death just like my Mom. My Uncle disappeared. The authorities said he fled to another country. He was involved in a whole lot of stuff. Drug dealing, money laundering, scamming women, you name it. I was in foster care for a little while until I could join the military."

"Do you ever think you'll hear from your Uncle again."

"I don't know. But my ears do perk up whenever I hear the name Cain and Mitchell mentioned in the same breath."

"Why?"

"Because I think he had something to do with the death of my Mom and my Aunt. I met him only once. Somehow, I felt if we connected, I would know if he was involved or not." I looked at the clock on the wall and it was eleven-fifty.

"Edward, It's almost twelve."

"It is, isn't it? Are you going to turn into a pumpkin now?" We both laughed.

"How about I make you feel like Cinderella?" He pulled my chin toward his lips and kissed me deep in my mouth. I had never felt anything like that before. This was way different than the immature kiss I received from Stew. It's as if I had left this world and flown to another one. It's the same way I felt in my dream. That kiss lingered and lingered. Without hesitation, I led Edward to my room where he stayed the night. The things I experienced that night were so frightening, yet delightful. My body took on movement and responses, I never knew it had.

Since I had made up my mind that I was going to live my life around Madelene without her knowing it, I had been to the Planned Parenthood Clinic and placed myself on birth control pills. When I did that, I had no intentions of sleeping with anyone anytime soon. I wanted to hold on to my virginity if I could, then sometimes I didn't. So, this night, this incredibly special night, I didn't. Edward was such a gentleman about the whole thing. He did something called "pull out" so that I would not be stuck "with child." I never told him I was on the pill because he would have thought I was running around sleeping with any and everybody.

He promised to write and keep in touch with me and thanked me for a wonderful evening. I thanked him for making me feel like a woman. It really didn't matter to me whether Edward kept in touch or not. He had shown me how to make love to a man and how to guide a man in making love to me right back. He was my first, a good first. I thought about when God sent me the right man to be my husband, it could only get better. Edward did call several times while he was still in the States but after six months, he was sent to Japan. I know he had a lot of growing up to do just like me. The good part about it is that he was male and there were fewer restrictions. Another good part, he was not my Mama's child—meaning he didn't have my same restrictions.

Chapter Seven
TWO MORE YEARS

It finally happened. Independence, sort of. Madelene followed me down to Liberty and helped me move into my dorm room. I had a roommate from Kerrville, TX by the name of Helen Brice.

Getting Settled In

Once Mama was gone and I had my side of the room organized the way I wanted it, it was time to explore. I had been on a brief tour of the campus prior to enrolling but now taking my time going inside every building, finding my classes, and buying my books would be pure joy. No Madelene looking over my shoulder, yet. The buildings were rather far apart so I knew when it came to eating lunch, I would have to hurry to get to my next class. Helen, although rather quiet, was a great help showing me around. She introduced me to some of her friends and they all seem friendly.

My Name Can't Bring No Shame!

One of the senior girls in the dorm was from Seawall. I didn't know her personally but I had seen her at several church events. Her name was Sherry. I don't remember her last name. Sherry also happened to be my Resident Advisor. She was like the dorm mom over my floor. The dorm also happened to be co-ed. Boys were on one side and girls on the other. I don't think Madelene realized that when we took the tour. I wasn't going to say a word. I'll admit, I was naïve about a lot of things. I felt like a country bumpkin that had just been let loose in the city. Other students that had been there, at least a year before me, started orientating me on college life. I had no idea that some of the orientating was a set up by Sherry to mar my name.

There was a resident advisor on the boy's side that went by the name Yum-Yum. I don't remember his real name but he was the first guy who befriended me. He seemed so nice and was showing me the ropes around campus. He walked me to every building so that I would know where my classes were. On the way back to the dorm early one evening, he asked if I wanted to go get a burger at Big Louie's Burger Joint just two blocks from the dorm. I was skeptical but I was also hungry, so I agreed.

About an hour later, we walked down to the burger place and had a seat. We talked about our hometowns and high school days, family, and friends back home. It was very innocent and informative. We walked back to the dorm—I went my way and he went his. I will never forget that when I entered my room, my phone was already ringing. I didn't know anyone so this puzzled me. There were at least three guys calling me and wanting to take me out. Helen was trying to tell me that these guys were calling me because I was new on campus. She said don't go anywhere with any of them because they are all dogs. Wow, a young person with Madelene's mentality.

Since I wanted to express real freedom, I ignored most of the invites but accepted one from a guy named Collin. He had been in the dorm lobby a couple of times and made small talk. He was rather quiet and seemed safe. Classes didn't start for me for another four days, so I agreed to go to this little hang out called the Classy Rooster. It served beer and sodas and some off the wall snacks. It was tiny but the music was good. We danced a little and talked a lot. Not many people were there probably because it was a Thursday. Everything was in walking distance so it made it easy to really communicate with a person as you are strolling along. As we walked up the steps to the dorm, Collin tried to kiss me.

"Whoa! I don't know you like that; we just barely met."

"Well according to Yum-Yum, you are hot and ready to go!"

"What? All I did with him was eat a burger!"

"According to him, you ate more than a burger!" I was so angry and so out done. I had no idea what Collin was talking about—ate more than a burger? Collin felt rejected and assumed that I didn't want to do anything with him because he was dark skin and Yum-Yum was light skinned. I assured him that the color of someone's skin doesn't have anything to do with my interest in them. I also told him don't bother calling my number ever again. I ran inside in tears. Sherry saw me on the way to the room.

"What's going on?"

"Sherry, somehow that resident advisor guy has told his guy friends that I am easy prey. I walked down to the Classy Rooster with this guy named Collin and when we returned, he tried to kiss me. Then, he told me that Yum-Yum told him I ate more than a burger with him!"

"Oh girl. They do all the new meat like that. They are harmless. Everybody knows they lie; you probably don't know a thing about giving head. You've been a little church girl all your life."

"Giving head?? What on earth is that?"

"Come on in my room girl. Let me school you." I spent at least two hours listening to the do's and don'ts of campus life. Who to casually friend and who not to friend at all. I appreciated her advice and felt as if she was like a Mom looking after all the freshmen girls that were living away from home for the first time. I still felt as if I had some unfinished business with that Yum-Yum Character. I went to his Supervisor and told him how he was scandalizing my name. He was angry and said that he would deal with him personally.

It was after dinner in the cafeteria and most of the students mingled around outside. I walked up to him and I pulled out the pocketknife that Madelene had given me as a going away present. I put it up to his cheek and said, "If you tell one more lie on me, I will cut your throat and shove your vocal chords up your ass! Do you understand me?"

"I don't know what you are talking about but I will have you thrown out of the dorm for this accusation!"

"Not before you get thrown out of your position. Your Supervisor has been notified. You better keep my name and any other filthy thing you want to attach to it out of your mouth and I mean that." I waved the blade quickly over his arm and made contact. It left a small thin mark but he ran off squealing like a pig.

"She cut me! That bitch cut me!"

The folks in the crowd were laughing and saying things like, "That's what you get." "You've met your match now, Yum." So on that day, I established myself as a good Christian girl with a knife. Things were going well or so I thought.

Almost Over and Out

My classes were easy to me and I was enjoying college life when it happened. It was discovered that Sherry called somebody at my church who called somebody that called somebody that called Madelene to tell her that I was on campus putting my mouth on boy's private parts. It was on a Saturday and I was in the lobby reading an assignment when in walks Madelene.

"Bring your ass here, you little slut. I'm going to beat your ass until it ropes like okra and you might as well start packing because you are going home!" I was in total shock. I was embarrassed. I was confused. Thank God Mrs. Graham heard all the commotion and came out of her office.

"Ma'am, may I help you?"

"Hell Naw! You can't do a damn thing for me except watch me pull my child out of this place."

"Well, as the immediate supervisor on the premises, the two of you must step into my office so that I can get that paperwork started." I knew withdrawal didn't work like that; a dorm mom could not withdraw you from school.

I remained quiet except for the semi-quiet sobbing I was doing. Once inside her office, Madelene who was anxious to fill out papers to withdraw me, started to calm down. Mrs. Graham pretended to look for them. She excused herself for a moment and went to the side storage room where all student files were kept. While inside that room, she made a phone call and found out that someone told Madelene what I was doing with boys on this campus and she was coming to half kill me and then take me out of this God forsaken place. With my student file in front of her, Mrs. Graham told Madelene that all of that was just rumors.

"The young man who started those rumors is now no longer enrolled here" (Wow, I didn't know he left. I just thought he was suspended.) She also told her that she and the other male supervisor did not tolerate that kind of nonsense from any student whether they were employed with the school or not.

"That young man has been a thorn in our side for a couple of years now. You have no worries with Bea or with the campus."

"Yeah, but someone from the church back home told me it was true."

"This is her student file and there is no report of such inappropriate behavior by Bea. I assure you, it is not true. Bea has applied to become a Resident Advisor and we do a thorough job when it comes to checking grades and character. She is going to be an asset to this campus. Please don't make her leave. She has done no wrong."

"Ok, I'll let her stay."

She turns to me and says, "But if I have to drive down here one more time because I heard you are not doing what you are supposed to do, you are out!"

"Yes, ma'am."

"By the way, you'll be proud to know that Bea defended herself quite well against her enemy. She pulled out a pocketknife on him and scared him to death—which she is not supposed to have on this campus, by the way. But due to the circumstances, she was not suspended and she must keep the weapon off her person at all times." Madelene's eyes lit up.

"She pulled her knife?"

"Indeed, she did. I assume she gets her fearlessness from you?"

"Yep, she gets that from me."

"I hope everything will be alright with you now, Mrs. Faye?"

"Oh, it's Stanford now. I was recently married." I sat in silence, feeling left out because I had no idea that she had gotten married. If that had of been me, wow!

After the meeting, we walked side by side without a word to the front of my dorm.

"I was going to tell you about Stanford and me next weekend when you were supposed to come home. But when all of this came up about what you were doing on this campus, I just put the information on the back burner."

"Congratulations! I am happy for you, Mama."

"It doesn't really matter whether you are happy for me or not, what's done is done."

"Do I have to come home next weekend because our Pre-Homecoming events begin then and I am helping with a fundraiser for the Children's Shelter."

"I suppose it'll be alright if you stay here. Besides, they are planning the Church Anniversary and I told Stanford I would meet with the Committee and help out if you didn't come home."

"Great, looks like we both have something to do next weekend."

"You just be sure that whatever you do, does not embarrass me or make me a grandma!"

"Yes, ma'am." With that, she walked to her car, opened the door and left. No…I love you, take care, nothing. But that was my Mom, that was who she was. I felt relieved that I would not have to go home because I had never experienced a college Pre-Homecoming or Homecoming before. I am sure it is going to be fun and I could use a little fun in my life right about now.

A New Experience

On the way inside, I say a flyer about a costume party happening on Friday. I think I should go. A new friend of mine, Margo, was a wardrobe major in the Theater Department. I needed her costuming expertise. She suggested that I go as Nefertiti, the Egyptian Queen and Great Royal wife of Akhenaten, an Egyptian Pharaoh. I loved the idea. I have always been culturally aware of my heritage so this costume was so me. When Margo was done, I looked regal and beautiful. I walked into the party with my head held high as if I had become this Egyptian Queen for real! The room stood still. Everyone was watching as I slowly walked to the center of the room searching for my throne. To the right of the room was an empty high back chair. I moved toward it with the intention of claiming it for the evening. But before I could reach it, a tall handsome man moved toward it and took a seat. I stood in front of him speechless and begin to turn and walk away.

"Oh Queen, I had no idea this was your seat. Come, sit down." He arose and offered me the throne. I felt so special. It was then that my mouth flew open when I zoomed in on his costume. He was dressed as a Pharaoh! What are the chances of that? Everyone there was dressed in various standardized costumes but it was only he and I that stood out.

"Allow me to introduce myself. My name is Tyreer (pronounced Tie Rear) Josephs."

"Pleased to meet you, Tyreer. My name is Bea Faye."

"Ah, that means that it would be most appropriate that I call you Queen Bee, correct?" We both laughed at the suggestion.

"I suppose that would be alright, at least for tonight anyway." Tyreer stood by my chair and chatted with me for what seemed like hours. We discussed our childhood, education, politics and how we fit in the scheme of it all.

"Would you care to dance? You've been sitting for a while."

"Yes, I would like that." We had been in our own little kingdom and now we were stepping out before the people. We took the dance floor by storm, dancing song after song until we almost dropped. Finally, a song came on that neither of us cared to dance to, so we headed towards the refreshment table. Tyreer was such a gentleman, sweet and kind. The party was coming to an end.

"I really have enjoyed your company Queen Bee and would be honored to continue our friendship, if that's alright with you, of course." He began to walk me to my car.

"Sure, that would be fine with me if we spent some time together and became friends."

"Very well, then. May I give you a call?" Of course, I had not one pen, pencil, or paper to write my phone number on.

"I'm sorry but I don't have anything with my number on it. If you wish to get in touch with me, I live in Lewis Hall just call the Hall and they will connect you to my room."

"I most certainly will." He opened my car door and made sure I was safely inside.

"You take care Queen; until we meet again." As I drove off, I tried to figure this guy out. I knew he was older, perhaps a senior, or not a student at all. He was mature and suave. Intelligent and respectful. Plus, he had a slight accent. I felt it was important that I find out just who Tyreer Josephs really was.

It May Be More Than It Appears

The next day, I finally took the time to check my mailbox. I received notification that I was officially a Resident Advisor. There was going to be a meeting held on Monday to train me for the job. Last night was a Nefertiti Fantasy Island type night for me but now it was over. I remained curious about Tyreer. Who was he? The weekend was all abuzz with Homecoming dances and parties but I chose only to attend the football game, where the final score was 50 to 14—we blew our opponents away. I volunteered to take an extra desk shift since I wasn't really interested in all the outside parties. So, I sat up front and studied for my Marketing exam. It was quiet because almost the entire dorm was empty except for me and about five other residents. My head was stuck in my book when a tall handsome gentleman walked up to the front desk. I stood up and there I was face-to-face with Tyreer.

"Hello, Queen. You told me I could find you here and I see I have succeeded."

"Tyeer, what a pleasant surprise. I was expecting a phone call perhaps but I am delighted you showed up in person."

"I showed up in person because I am hoping you take our friendship personally."

"But of course."

"It is obvious that you are working but when will you be free? I would love to take you to lunch or dinner."

"I am free after church tomorrow which will be around twelve noon."

"Great, then it is lunch tomorrow around one o'clock?"

"Yes, that is fine."

"Very well. I will pick you up here and we will go to Cloe's for lunch."

"Ok, I will look forward to it." I watched as he walked away with a confident swag and thought, what does he want with me? I had heard that Cloe's was an elegant steakhouse about ten miles south of the campus. Students went there on special occasions like formal events or weddings. Most students could not afford to eat there on a regular basis, so I knew this man was not a student. I became more anxious to find out as much as I could about Tyreer. Since there was no Google back then, I had to rely on newspapers and people who knew him, criminal records or teachers and professors who might know him.

After my shift, I headed to the campus library. I found prior yearbooks for the campus and begin to search photos and faculty. It turned out that Tyreer was quite a football star and was well respected on campus. Counting back from his senior year up until now would make him six years older than me. I knew he wasn't a student. His present position was that as Student Recruiter for all the campuses affiliated with the University system. He had been responsible for giving out scholarships and keeping the enrollment above and beyond expectations for over three years now.

My Madelene side popped up: But how did he do it? Did he bribe parents? Did they promise to let him have sex with their daughters in trade for full time education? What? Once that side emerged, I became fearful and untrusting. I was cancelling Cloe's on tomorrow. But I didn't have his number. I had to find a Faculty Directory. Oh, wait a minute, that won't work either—it was Saturday, all administrative offices were closed. I started to panic. Then, I prayed and asked the

Lord to help me to turn him down gently on tomorrow; not to appear crazy or double-minded. But after all the things we talked about that night, he never mentioned what he did for a living. I tossed and turned most of the night wondering how Sunday after church would play out. I couldn't rehearse what I was going to say because I had no idea as to what I was going to say. Sunday came too soon.

A Divine Coincidence

After church, I didn't change into the dress I was going to wear since I wasn't going. I threw on a casual jumpsuit and waited in the lobby for Tyreer to show up. There was no large gap in time between the time I arrived back to the dorm and the time he showed up. I saw him walk up the steps and I almost stopped him at the door. But I didn't because I was in complete shock. He had someone I knew very well from back home with him. It was Sis. Niece, well Mother Niece now. What was she doing with him? He looked a little ashamed for me because of how casually I was dressed. He was in a suit and tie and Mother Niece had on her Sunday best in Purple with matching hat. I was so embarrassed.

"Bea, I'd like to introduce you to my Mother, Maggie Niece. She says she knows you." Mother Niece looked to be about seventy years old now but she still remembered me from the District Congress and Convention days. That lady made a big difference in my Christian journey and here she was standing in front of me with her son, Tyreer.

"She does. If it hadn't been for your Mother, I would not have become as strong in the Word of God as I am now." I gave her a hug and a kiss on the cheek.

"How have you been Mother Niece?"

"I've been doing well in my old age by the grace of God. Tyreer mentioned your name and I instantly demanded that he take me on this lunch date just so I could see you."

"Oh, that is so sweet Mother Niece. I love you so much."

"I love you so much too, baby. Now, when are we going to eat?"

"I won't be but a few minutes. I ran overtime scheduling for next week. You guys have a seat, I'll be right back." I hurried back to my room where the dress I intended to wear was still lying across the bed. My hair was still in good shape so in about ten minutes I was ready to go.

Once we were at the dinner table chatting about things back home and how Tyreer and I met, I had one question that I had to ask Mother Niece.

"Mother Niece, why is it that I have known you all of my life but never knew about Tyreer?"

"Dear, I am sorry to say but Tyreer was raised by his father after his Dad and I divorced. My second husband and I had two other sons, Ralph and Jonah, those are the two you know."

"Oh, I see." I was trying to wrap my head around the fact that someone could ever bring themselves to divorce such a sweet woman like her. Or what kind of monster did she marry that caused her to divorce him? *(Up pops Madelene again: What if Tyreer's Dad was mean with a bad temper? Perhaps that's why he hadn't been married yet at almost thirty. What if.)* STOP IT! JUST STOP IT! MADELINE GET OUT OF MY HEAD!

"Mom, I found Bea to be such a breath of fresh air. Perhaps it wasn't meant for us to meet until now."

"How's Madelene, Bea?"

"Doing well, thanks for asking. She is remarried now to Deacon Stanford from True Way Baptist Church."

"What you say! Well, good for her. Tell her I said, 'Congratulations' when you see her."

"Yes, ma'am. I sure will." The evening was nice and moved at a calm slow pace. I enjoyed seeing Mother Niece again but if I had changed my mind on my own about going on this date, I think I would have wanted it to be just the two of us. At the end of the evening, I watched as he took his time making sure his Mom was seated comfortably and all strapped in. It seemed as if everything he did for her was out of love. And with every response from her, there was love returned.

Tyreer drove up to my dorm, opened my door and walked me to the front door of the building. He gave me a friendly hug and said that he would be in touch. I waved goodbye to both and went inside to be alone with my thoughts. What were the chances that I meet a guy that I already knew his parent and respected her to the moon and back? This guy came from good stock.

Just Ask

Resident Advisor paperwork, class assignments, projects, it was all becoming so overwhelming. I really needed a break but I didn't have the funds or the time to take one. If I could just get a full Friday to Monday off, it would help. At this point, I might would go home. Especially since I had not heard from Tyreer since that night at Cloe's.

I prayed to God for some relief. I felt as if I was becoming burned out. In a daze, I sat at that front desk trying to juggle everything I had going on. I had to deal with complaints about roommates, enforce curfew and maintain a 3.8 GPA. Whew! I was exhausted. This one student kept bugging me about changing roommates when I kept telling her she would have to contact housing about that. I had no authority to change anybody's roommate, I served as an RA and Front Desk Clerk only.

"Then what good are you then! You're just a nobody; a waste of time and money!" Madelene, I mean, I reached out to grab her in her collar when in steps Tyreer. In a soft low tone, I told her that I was sorry that she felt that way and I would make sure the Supervisor would be informed of her complaint. That seemed to appease her somewhat and she walked away.

"Hello there, Mr. Josephs."

"Hi Bea. I know I haven't contacted you since that night but Mom fell and I had to stay with her until someone from home health care was assigned to assist her while I was away. I had an important recruiting engagement in Florida and time slipped away. You forgive me?" (No not really)

"Of course, you're a busy man."

"Bea, you don't seem to be your usual happy self. Is there anything wrong?"

"No, not really. I'm tired, I suppose."

"It sounds like you could use a break of some sort. Is there any way I could help you with that?"

"Sure, if you could find someone to take my weekend shift, finish my assignments and then swoop me off to some quiet island—that would be great."

"I will see what I can do." He grinned, reached over the counter and gave me a soft kiss on the cheek.

"I'll be in touch." Yea, his famous last words. Who cares, anyway? I have enough on my plate besides trying to figure out what Tyreer's motive is. The weekend drug on. I was considering not going to any of my classes on Monday just so I could get some rest. It was around eight pm on Sunday evening when I finally took a shower, a breath and curled up in bed with a bag of almost stale popcorn. My phone rang and it was Tyreer on the other end of the line.

"Bea, how are you?"

"I'm ok. I'm just still tired."

"Well, I have great news for you."

"Really?"

"Yes, I pulled some strings with the President of the University who just happens to be an old golf buddy of mine. I convinced him to give you next week off so that you could fly back to Florida with me. I told him since you were majoring in PR and Marketing what a great experience this would be for you. You'd be able to see how the University system handles recruitment and PR all at the same time. So, what do you think?" I was shocked beyond a response. (*Madelene kicked in: "You are so stupid. Don't you fall for this trip. All he wants to do is get in your drawers and take advantage of you. If you can't pay to go, don't go!*)

"Wow! Uh, I don't know what to say. I appreciate it and all but if I can't pay my own way, I'd better stay put."

"Bea, the University is picking up the tab. It's all a part of my budget, you would owe nothing. Look, you said you needed a break and I know it's not an Island but it's the best I could do."

"Well, can I think about it?"

"Sure but our flight leaves at two pm next Monday afternoon."

"What about my classes for that week?"

"It's called school business leave and you will have extra time to make up assignments once you return. Let me know what you decide. I will contact you again soon."

Oh Lord! Oh Lord! I don't know what to do. Madelene would try and kill me right after she called me a whore. *Good Christian girls do not go nowhere on no trip with a man that they are not married or engaged to.* Maybe she's right. I know, I'll call him back and ask about sleeping arrangements. While I was in thought as to how to approach the subject, the phone rang again.

"Oh, and Bea, you will have your own room in a student section on the campus. They put recruiters up in a different building just in case you were concerned."

"Oh, alright. Thanks; talk to you soon."

I felt so much better. This man went to a lot of trouble to give me a break and it would be a great experience. It was school business and I am grown enough to handle myself and school business even if it was in another state. I had never been out of Texas so this would also be a bonus. Should I call Mama and tell her? Nah! So, I agreed to take the trip. I knew once we were going to be in separate rooms, I would go.

Suddenly, I became excited and energy came out of thin air. I waited about an hour and called Tyreer back and told him I would be ready by twelve-thirty on next Monday to go to the airport.

The week flew by. Once there, we boarded a small plane that flew into Mason Airport and then on to Florida. He and I talked and laughed almost the entire trip until I dozed off in mid conversation. I was embarrassed when I opened my eyes and found him smiling and staring at me. I apologized and of course, he assured me there was no need. He really was such a gentleman the whole time. I really, really liked him. Was the feeling mutual? Regardless, I had to think about what this trip would mean for me, for my career—whether the feeling was mutual or not. I have a once in a lifetime opportunity to learn and study from the best in the business. If a committed relationship does not come out of this, I won't be angry; still thankful. I will always give God the glory for whatever He does in my life, regardless of the way I want it to go. When I look back over my life and I think about how I wanted things to go, I wonder if I would have been better off with my other siblings and my real mother? Would I have had as good of an education that I have now? I don't know. I just wish I could have known.

Chapter Eight
IN A FEW MORE YEARS

When we arrived at the University in Florida, it was just as he said it would be. I was housed in an Administrative Suite that had student living quarters attached to it on the second and third floors. My suite was so beautiful with all the high-class executive amenities. It was where the Resident Supervisors, who traveled from campus to campus, lodged.

Tyreer informed me that there would be a dinner meeting in two hours that I needed to attend. It would clarify what was going to take place the following day and the rest of the week. Dinner was set for seven and I was so excited—I almost dressed way too early. This is the type of business I wanted to be a part of—this is what I lived for.

I made myself calm down and didn't put on my little black dress until six-fifteen. The meeting was going to be held in the same building where I was staying, inside one of the huge ballrooms.

Just Can't Seem To Get Away

The phone in my room rang. I was sure it was Tyreer telling me he would be waiting for me downstairs. I answered with a smile in my voice.

" itch! What do you think you are doing leaving the State without letting me know, and with a grown ass man at that!" Oh No! How did she know? How did she find out? I said nothing. Stay calm, Bea. You have an important dinner meeting and you must make a good impression.

"Mom, is everything alright?"

"Well, if it wasn't alright you wouldn't be around to do nothing about it. After all I've done for you… worked my fingers to the bone cleaning folks' houses and raising they kids,,,and your little sneaky whorish ass have nerve enough to sneak away with God knows who."

"Mama, it is school business. I was invited to learn how to market and recruit for the University. This would look good on my resume' and would open doors for me to get hired at a good PR firm."

"If it is school business, then why aren't you being supervised?'

"This is college, not high school. The Executive Director over recruiting is mentoring me and is the one that asked the President of the University if I could come along for the experience. Since it is school business the University is paying for the entire trip. Isn't that great?"

"Oh, I see! This man rigs up a free trip for you so that he can ask you to sleep with him in return; nothing is ever free. I have told you that repeatedly but you are stupid and a hoe just like your Mama was!"

"Who is this man anyway and how do you know him?"

"I met him at a Homecoming event. He is a complete gentleman and has not tried to take me to bed or even suggest it; besides, he comes from good stock."

"Good stock? What in the hell is that supposed to mean? What? Is he a chicken?"

"No, he's Sis. Niece's eldest son."

"Maggie Niece, from the church?"

"Yes, ma'am." I would have given anything to see her face through the phone that day because I knew it had egg on it. She respected Sis. Niece especially since she practically raised me up in every church event imagined.

"Hump! Why nobody never knew about this so-called eldest son?"

"After she and Tyreer's father divorced, Tyreer chose to live with his father and that is who raised him."

"If his Daddy raised him and don't nobody know who his Daddy is, then how can you determine he came from good stock? Huh Miss Sassy? Tell me that!"

"Because Sis. Niece is his mother." Silence. I wanted to say so bad like a kid on a playground: 'What's the matter, cat got your tongue!' After about sixty seconds, I asked her again if she was alright. She wanted to know why I was asking her that question.

"Because with the job I have on campus, we must leave names and phone numbers to our locations. This is in case of an emergency. The Supervisor then locates or gives the number to the family member to reach the person that needs to be informed of the emergency."

"Oh. Uh well, it was an emergency. I had called your room 100 times and I wasn't getting an answer. Unlike you, I was worried about you and wanted to know if you were alright."

"Yes but the policy is that something had to have happened to a family member not that someone was just worried about somebody."

"Ok, so I lied. I told them I was in the hospital and I needed to reach you right away. So there. But I don't give a damn if he is the eldest son of Jesus Christ, he better not put his hands on you in a nasty way. I will blow up Niece's house and everybody in it if he does. You understand me? And you are not staying down there a whole week. You better have your ass back on that campus by Wednesday or else I am pulling you out of that place!"

"But Mama, the University seminar is paid through the entire week."

"And? I don't care if they paid through next year. You better be back on that campus on Wednesday like I said. You are not going to embarrass me living a lose life, traveling with a grown man, not even a student and thinking he ain't going to try and get in your panties. You are so damn stupid! Wednesday!" She slammed the phone down. The phone rang as soon as she hung up.

"Bea, are you ready? I'm on my way to walk you to the ballroom." I spoke almost in a whisper.

"Yes, I'm ready." Once again, Madelene had ruined my evening just like she was on a mission to ruin my entire life. I quickly wiped the tears off my face and matted a little face powder over where they had streamed.

After that phone call, I wanted to pack my things and leave right away. I had to find a way to tell Tyreer I needed to be back by Wednesday. After the demand from Madelene I felt defeated, again. I knew I had to make a good impression but I just didn't know if I could. I began to pray and ask God to change my frame of mind, put a smile on my face and let the evening go smoothly. He answered my prayer.

Once the dinner was over, Tyreer walked me back to my room. I stood there trying not to tear up. I told him about the conversation with Madelene and that I had to be back on campus by Wednesday or else she would pull me out of the school. A small smile came across his face. At first, I thought he was making light of my misery.

"You find this humorous in some way?"

"Not at all. It's just that I am way ahead of you."

"What do you mean?"

"Do you remember when I left the table to take a phone call?"

"Yes, OH NO! Don't tell me it was my MOTHER!"

"Calm down. No, it was not your Mother, but mine."

"Huh?"

"I am sure you told your Mom who I was and who my Mother happens to be. So, she gave her a call to verify and to give her a piece of her mind about her old a— son taking her daughter away without her permission to do who knows what to her. My Mother obviously knows your Mom well. she calmed her down, assured her that you were safe with me and nothing bad would happen to you."

"Really?" I started to have hope that I would be able to stay the entire week.

"Does that mean I will be able to stay all week?"

"No. My Mom promised her I'd have you back on campus by Wednesday and I will. All that means is that you will have to glean all that you can the next couple of days before returning. I've already contacted University Travel and you will fly out first thing

Wednesday before your Mom can drive to the campus to check and see if you are there."

"Uh, don't be so sure about that!" We chuckled at the idea of it all.

"Tyreer, I want to thank you for being so understanding and I apologize for all the drama."

"Not to worry. It's just that you are her pride and joy, and she wants to protect you from the evils of this world." I stood in deep thought thinking, then why am I not protected from her?

Tyreer gave me a soft kiss on my hand and bid me goodnight. Did he like me? Was there a hidden agenda? Lord, just show me but first let me rest.

The next couple of days were fast and furious. I learned a lot but before I knew it, I was on a plane headed back to the campus. I thought about the things that took place and how Tyreer planted a seed of understanding in me. Perhaps Madelene behaved the way she did because I was her pride and joy but she just didn't know how to show it.

It Happened So Fast

Wednesday afternoon I decided to sit in the lobby and do some reading. I couldn't believe how many assignments were due from the past three days. I was the only one out in the lobby besides the new freshman Desk Clerk who had zero people skills. Buried in my Marketing Strategies Manual, I never saw her standing beside me.

"Mama?"

"Yeah, it's me. I'm tired as all get out but I wasn't going to let this day go by until I saw for myself if you came back like I said."

"Yes, ma'am. I'm here."

"If you expect to stay here, I better not catch you with that old a Tyler, Terry, or whatever his name is again. You could have ruined your reputation running off with that man. I don't care who his Mama is!"

"Mama, it wasn't a vacation. It was school business and I really learned a lot."

"You better learn how to learn a lot right here on this campus or else you are coming home. Do you understand me?"

"Yes."

"Yes. Yes!" She raised her hand and slapped me across my face so hard until I fell backwards off the chair I was sitting in and blacked out. When I opened my eyes, I was in the campus infirmary with the Physician's Assistant (PA) and Campus Security staring at me.

"Bea. Bea. Can you hear me?"

"Yes, I can hear you." My eyes were blurry and my head was hurting so bad. The PA told me that I must have nodded off and fell backwards in my chair because the Senior RA came through the lobby and found me on the floor.

"Do you remember what happened?" I looked around and Madelene was nowhere to be found.

"The last thing I remember is that I was talking to my Mother and then I woke up here."

"Talking to your Mother? Where is she?"

"I don't know but she was here. OW, my head!"

"Bea, you've had a pretty hard fall so we are going to keep you overnight for observation. Maybe things will be clearer for you in the morning. If not, we might have to transfer you to General. We will call home and let your Mother know what happened."

"She knows what happened, she was here. I answered her in what she calls a disrespectful way and she slapped me so hard until I fell off my chair." They both looked at me as if I made the whole thing up.

"Ok Bea, get some rest now." They turned the lights off and in the still darkness I kept thinking how she could do this to me and then disappear. Yep, I was her pride and joy alright, which she so easily could deny. The best thing about that entire incident was that there was no one to witness it. That worked in her favor. I was still lying in the infirmary the next morning when the campus MD, Dr. Clark, walked in.

"I hear you had a tough fall. Do you remember how it happened?" I had awakened in the middle of the night with the decision not to try and convince anyone that my Mother did this to me, so I told him I didn't really remember.

"Last night's staff said you seemed to think that your Mother had something to do with it, yet she was nowhere to be found. No one saw her on campus or in the dorm."

"I'm sorry, like you said it was a tough fall." Your scans and x-rays are clear. How is your head feeling this morning?"

"I feel a little drowsy with a mild headache but nothing I can't handle."

"If you are sure of that then I will release you to go back to your dorm. Stay there and rest for today, then resume classes tomorrow."

"Yes sir, Dr. Clark, will do." I headed toward the dorm, feeling hopeless, trapped, unloved, and mistreated. I thought college would be my answer to getting away from Madelene and living a wonderful, peaceful life. But now I knew with her controlling my life, there would never be peace.

This Can't Be Real

Tyreer seemed to avoid me after my having to leave the conference early to come back to campus due to Madelene's command. I started to call him but Madelene would say I was desperate and acting like my real Mom, so I didn't.

At least two weeks had passed and things seemed to be back to some sense of normal. I went to class every day, made good grades and even picked up a couple of marketing scholarships that provided my bare necessities. Madelene only contacted me once after the incident and that was to tell me that she and Dec. Stanford were having problems and they may not be together much longer. I listened and thought to myself, I'm surprised he lasted this long. Of course, she warned that she could pop up anytime and that I better not be caught with a man or a boy or else I would be beat within an inch of my life. Nothing had changed. I guess I thought being away would make her miss me and love me more, it didn't. Tyreer finally came around and gave me the pity speech about how sorry he felt for me but after all it was my Mother and I needed to respect her.

"We just don't know how long we are going to have them around Bea. We must cherish them while they are here." I agreed with him in part but Sis. Niece was easy to cherish. She was sweet and kind, loving and giving, spiritual and fair. None of the traits that my Mom had, at all.

We dated quietly. Some weekends, I would go to his home. It was so gorgeous and he had made most of the furniture himself. He was handsome, intelligent, and gifted with industrial arts skills. He was so nice to me. Since he was older, I think he thought he should look out for me and he did. If he were around and some jock tried to hit on me in an inappropriate way, he would speak to him man to man. Yet, if they asked him if I was his woman, he never affirmed the question. Noticing the respect and prestige he had on campus, being non-titled didn't really bother me. Therefore, we carried on as a couple, off campus.

These two years at Liberty were flying by. I was now a Senior Resident Advisor at Ellis Hall. There was a mid-semester orientation being held at the Student Union Building that I had to attend. It was my responsibility to recruit as many freshmen as I could to reside at Ellis. The other dorms were represented by the Student Recruitment Staff spear headed by Tyreer. They were there to welcome the new students and to assist them in making "away from home" adjustments.

Although I didn't want to admit it, it bothered me that Tyreer and I could not go public with our relationship. I suggested it was best that way in case my Mom decided to do one of her pop-ups. But deep down inside, I wanted the world to know that I was his lady and he was my man. Other than a nod or a smile or two in public, it was as if I never existed in his life. I took it upon myself to snoop around to see if he was seeing someone else. A girlfriend and I would make a random drive by on his street to see if an additional car had parked at his house. Sometimes, we would linger parked down the street to see if anyone would emerge. After a while, this strategy began to feel inadequate because he could have gone and picked her up. I decided to take the spying into my own hands.

One night when I couldn't sleep about four am, I parked down the street and waited until the break of dawn to see if a female would appear from his residence that had spent the night. The only one who appeared was Tyreer. He emerged in some shorts and a t-shirt to take his trash out. I started to back my car in reverse for fear he might see me and ran into a neighbor's trash can. I saw him look in my direction so I ducked down beneath the steering wheel so he couldn't see me. I remained very still and managed to peep up high enough to see he had gone back inside. I felt silly and stupid, then I felt angry. If there was no one else, why couldn't other people know we were seeing each other, pop up or no pop up? And why when he protected me from other men did he not acknowledge me as his lady? I turned the car around, it was six am and I had an eight o'clock class. Question after question kept popping up in my mind. I came to learn that these were Madelene's questions and insecurities embedded in me. But perhaps I learned too late.

Death Happens

There was going to be a large end of the semester ball for outgoing Seniors. I felt nervous and afraid to ask Tyreer if he would escort me to the ball. If he didn't want to be seen with me on campus, how would he say yes to escorting me to the ball? Deep in thought, my phone rang. I was hoping it was him because it had been almost two weeks since I had been invited over. It was Madelene. What was she up to now? I was back. I was on campus. I was doing what I was supposed to do.

"Bea, you will have to come home as soon as you can. Deacon Stanford just passed away!"

"What? How?"

"He had a heart attack and I just can't handle all of this by myself, come home!!"

"But Mom, I have finals coming up and graduation is only two weeks away. I would have to get permission to come home under those circumstances."

"Then get it! School is almost out anyway right."

"Yes, but like I said, finals and graduation are coming up and if I am not available to take the exams that would mean that my graduation could be delayed."

"So, then it's delayed! I really don't care how you do it, just do it. Bring your ass home and I mean it!" She hung up.

Tears fell like rain. I had worked so hard to maintain a 3.8 GPA while working and even sometimes tutoring. She didn't care whether I graduated or not. She didn't care about my life in the present and she was not concerned about my future. I began to pray for lack of knowing what else to do. I asked God to give her strength to carry on without me at least until I could take all my exams. If I didn't walk across the stage, I could live with that. But not having the exam finals to boost my GPA to a 4.0 was unbearable to me. I stayed on my knees for at least an hour begging the Lord to show me what to do and how to do it.

Morning came quickly. I had bags under my eyes, and I didn't bother to groom myself as I usually do. I headed toward the Dean's Office that handled my degree plan. Usually, the Dean would not see you unless you had an appointment but Dean James knew me and he knew my Mother from way back when. I knocked on his door.

"Come in."

"Dean James."

"Why Bea, how are you? I've been keeping up with you on paper and you are doing a fine job young lady. As a matter of fact, I was speaking with some of the Board members the other day and suggested to them that you would be an excellent candidate for our Master's in Business Program on full scholarship. What do you think about that Bea"? I just stood and cried; I couldn't speak. Here I was on the brink of not graduating with honors as an Undergrad but God placed it on this man's heart to see that I receive a Master's degree. God loved me so much. Why didn't my Mother love me this much?

"Are you ok? Here sit down and tell me what's going on."

When I composed myself, I began to tell him my story. How I was commanded to come home so close to graduation and during final exams. Between all the sniffling, babbling, and snorting and a half a box of Kleenex, I was silent.

"Bea, don't you worry. I will contact your professors and let them know you have a family emergency. They will prepare your exams early and you will take them with you. When they are completed, you will mail them back to each of them. Do you think that is possible?"

"Yes, sir. But what about graduation itself."

"That I can't delay. The University can always mail your diploma to you should you not make it back in time to walk the stage. I know that every graduate looks forward to taking that final step at the end of any degree of study."

"Yes sir, I really do."

"All I can offer you at this point is that you try and make it back. If not, we will send it by mail. I'm sorry Bea."

"No problem. Arranging for me to complete my finals at home is more than enough. I thank you from the bottom of my heart."

"I know you do Bea. I know you do."

I walked out of his office feeling better but still defeated by the power of M. I called her and told her I would be home in forty-eight hours. I told her what Dean James had done for me and how grateful I was that he helped me out. She seemed quiet, different. Perhaps grief? With her, you could never be sure. I was dreading this with all that was within me but I knew I had to be there for her. She was still my Mom. The only one I knew.

I Feel Sorry For Her

There was no exaggeration in the statement that she could not handle all of this. Finding insurance papers, contacting relatives, contacting the funeral home, planning the program, I did it all and I was wiped out. Most of the time, Madelene seemed subdued. She didn't have much to say and she allowed me to handle everything without demand or interruption. I knew she didn't read very well or understand legal jargon so as I read, I had to explain. A lot of things she wanted to fuss about but she couldn't because she had no idea as to what she would be fussing about.

The day of the services arrived, and I must say between taking those exams and doing all the mental labor for Deke's assent into

Glory, I was lifeless. I couldn't wait to get back to the dorm for some peace and rest. I kept the service program short and sweet and to my advantage, I scheduled everything so that I could get back in time to graduate.

In a way, I hated leaving her. For the first time, I saw her not strong but hurt. Not loud but quiet. Not demanding but humble. I can't be sure but to me she had to be thinking long and hard about death, especially since her husband had died lying beside her. That had to be tough. Yet, she never shed one tear. But was she crying inside and too afraid to let her feelings show on the outside? It's strange what people will do just to keep up a front or a reputation. For God's sake woman, this was your husband! Or did you not feel the need to show him love like he showed you? Like you never showed me?

During the repass, neighbors, church members, family and friends all offered their sincere condolences. I stepped away from her side to go to the ladies' room. When I went inside, I heard two women talking to each other in the stalls. It was about Madelene.

"She probably ran the poor man crazy with all of her demands and rules. He seemed nice enough but what he saw in that mean old hag, I'll never know."

"Me either, girl. I bet he's glad he's dead and at home with the Lord instead of at home with Madelene Faye!"

I turned around and walked out. I lost the urge to go after that. I really felt bad about the way other people felt about my Mama. But I also knew that everything they said about her was the truth. She didn't make friends easy, she hardly ever smiled and she had a mean spirit. Everybody knew that. In a way, I think she wanted everybody to know to protect herself. Being a mean bully meant that you did not have to be bothered with folks. They would never know that you drank beer or made your daughter strip so you could whoop the blood out of her; held her head underwater 'till she couldn't breathe and they certainly didn't know that she courted married men. Yep, the fewer people around her, the less they knew about her. And Heaven forbid if you tried to show or tell her the error of her ways. She accepted instructions from no one. If she told you to do something, she expected you to do it. But if you told her to do something, she wanted to beat you, shoot you, or cut you. Everyone was afraid of my Mama—preachers, teachers, doctors, lawyers, and cops. Everybody!

I wanted to try and understand what kind of person she was on the inside. Her exterior was certainly threatening, her statue strong and her expressions were rough. I often pondered about a different person inside, though. Was she a fearful not fearless individual that had suffered some sort of traumatic experience as a child that she just couldn't let go of? Was it a really bad experience—one that caused her to hate men, hate people and from the way I felt, hate me? Yes, I felt sorry for her because hatred and bitterness controlled her life.

Chapter Nine
AFTER THE BALL

As fate would have it, the ball had been rescheduled because there was a fire at the selected venue. Therefore, they had to choose another one, so now, the date was delayed. Oh No! That means I still had time to ask Tyreer to escort me to this final event of my undergraduate career. But how? Why? I had not heard a word from him. Why should he be privileged to escort me to the ball? Perhaps, I won't go after all. The ball is on Saturday of next week and graduation on the following Monday. Yeah, that's it. I won't go. I must pack to return home for the summer and start to look for a job. Even if I could convince Madelene to let me come back and work on my Masters, I would still need income during the summer months. So, it's settled. No attending the Graduation Ball, that way I won't need an escort. I will ask to work the desk while other students attend. That will be a little more cash in my account to survive on while I find work back home.

The Talk

I was completely happy and satisfied with my decision until Tyreer called. He said he had something he needed to talk to me about. I could not imagine what it could be. I agreed to meet him in the courtyard in about an hour. It was an early spring evening and it was pleasant outside.

"Well…Hello, Stranger." I greeted him between a smirk and a smile.

"Bea, I've missed you." (You sure have a funny way of showing it.) "I know you probably don't believe that (no, I don't) but I really do."

"That's nice, Tyreer. I don't know if you noticed or not but I am almost out of here. In two weeks, I will be gone back to sad Seawall, living with my Mom over the summer until I can either come back to school or find a decent job. So, if you missed me less than two and a half miles away from your house, I think it's safe to say, you are really going to miss me now."

"Ok, I deserved that. But that is what I wanted to talk to you about."

"Graduation? Going back home? The way you keep me a secret. Which one?"

"Perhaps all of them. Bea, I have been offered a position in Nitsville as head of Student Services for NVU. It is the opportunity I have been praying for and I have accepted the position."

"Congratulations Tyreer! God does answer prayer. I know that you will be successful and guide a lot of students to their careers. Now if you'll excuse me, I have to get back to work." I began to walk away.

"Bea, I wasn't finished with our conversation."

"What more is there to this conversation? You prayed for a position. You were offered the position. You accepted the position and you are leaving. So how is the conversation not over?"

"Because I want you to go with me."

"Go with you?? Are you crazy!?!? What kind of person do you think I am?? I thought you had more respect for me than that Tyreer! I thought you were different. There is no way I would move to Nashville with you without being married. I just wasn't raised that way!" He went down on one knee, pulled out a velvet blue box and began to speak.

"Bea, I do respect you and I love you. I want to marry you and take you with me. Bea Coral Faye, will you marry me?" I was too afraid to say yes and loved him too much to say no. I didn't know what to say, so tears ran down my cheeks.

"Well, will you?" I knew that I was going to catch hell from Madelene if I said yes.

"Yes, yes. I will!" He placed the most beautiful two carat Princess cut diamond ring on my finger. I couldn't believe that I was engaged to a handsome, intelligent, successful and loving man. I was on cloud nine.

Tyreer said that he would be leaving right after my graduation to start moving into the four-bedroom, four-bathroom house that was part of his benefit package. Students would not need his assistance until early August, so I suggested getting married mid-July.

"That will be fine. Whatever you want. I know this is your first wedding and all I want to suggest is that you keep it under ten thousand. dollars. That is the budget, ok." I almost fainted. That was more than enough for what I had in mind. I wanted to discuss what my role would be besides Tyreer Josephs' wife. He was way ahead of me.

"Oh, and if you decide you want to pursue your Master's, you would be able to do so tuition free at NVU." This man! He had thought of everything. Now, the business of breaking the news to Madelene.

"Bea, I know how your Mother can be so I would like to be with you when we tell her the great news. As a matter of fact, I will bring my Mom along and we can share the news with our mothers at the same time. I can't wait to share the news with the two most important people in our lives."

My heart melted at the fact that he wanted to share the news with both but fear was arising. Madelene would use this opportunity to show out and embarrass both of us. I had to muster up the courage to become a woman. A woman separated from the commands of her and become the wife Tyreer needed me to be. I had to make that dreaded phone call. *'Lord, please be with me.'*

"Mom, how are you?"

"I guess I am alright considering I just lost my husband and I am here all alone by myself trying to deal with the loss."

"Just know that I have been praying for you." "Okay, what are you really trying to tell me?"

"Tyreer, his mother and I would like to come and talk with you. Would this upcoming weekend be alright?"

"Talk to me about what??!! You damn well better not be pregnant because I will shoot that no good old ass man and rip that baby right out of your belly and never look back!" I tried not to lose control, so I responded softly.

"Of course, not Mom. You raised me better than that."

"I sure in the hell did! So, why you are bringing these folks to my house?"

"It's a surprise. Please tell me it's ok that we come down."

"I guess but don't come to stay all day. I am going fishing later that afternoon and I don't want to be held up."

"Oh, you won't. Is nine o'clock alright?"

"Yeah, that's alright but ya'll need to be gone by twelve."

I couldn't figure out why she was so specific on the time. She had never done that before. Turns out, what I didn't know then but I know now, is that she was seeing a man in the neighborhood and Deacon Stanford's body was barely cold. That told me that she was more than likely seeing this man while she was MARRIED! Later, I found out he was married, too!

"Great, thanks for letting us come down Mom. I'll talk to you later." I hung up the phone before she could change her mind.

I called Tyreer to let him know we were scheduled for the next Saturday at nine am at my Mom's house. He had no problem with it at all and was excited to share the news. Me, I was terrified at what might take place. But if I was ever going to be bold and brave and break away from her clutches, now was the time. I had to do this. The week drug on and my nerves were just about unhinged. Tyreer called to confirm that he would be around to pick me up at eight-fifteen. All I could think about was what Madelene might do when she heard the news. *'Dear God, please don't let this woman hurt anyone physically or emotionally during this meeting. If she needs to hurt anyone, let it be me. I'm used to it. Amen.'*

The Meeting

Sis. Niece and I chit-chatted on the way and talked about my young oratory days. The conversation switched to what type of wedding I wanted to have and how many people I wanted to invite.

"I actually hadn't thought about it in depth just yet. I'm still glowing from the proposal." I gently touched Tyreer's hand.

"Alright dear, but you must start thinking about those things soon. July will be here before you know it. Tyreer has a huge network of friends and I'm sure they would all want to attend."

"Mom, that doesn't mean that they have to attend. Some may not want to. Besides, the wedding is for the bride; it's her day. If Bea wants 25 guest or 250 guest, it's fine with me."

"Oh, isn't he such a sweet boy, Bea?"

"Yes Sis. Niece, he sure is."

"You can call me Mother Niece, dear. After all we are going to be family."

Family, huh? That didn't sound familiar to me. The family environment I came from was so unkind and dysfunctional. I didn't know what it was like to be around real family. All families had issues and most kids had issues with their parents; yet, they still loved one another and found ways to show it. They would apologize, hug, and reassure one another that they loved each other no matter what. I hadn't experienced that. The closest I came to that love scenario was Papa, someone she completed subtracted from my presence.

"Why thank you, Mother Niece and I am delighted to become a part of your family."

"I'm delighted too, Bea. I'm delighted too." Pulling up in my Mothers' driveway, I was surveying the premises, making sure no firearms were visible. She came outside to greet us with a crooked smile.

"Hello, come on in." Mama greeted Mother Niece and shook Tyreer's hand. Now, I was really scared.

"I'm sure Bea told you that I have a fishing trip planned for this afternoon, so what was it you needed to talk to me about?" Tyreer took the lead.

"Mrs. Stanford, I've grown very fond of your daughter and…"- Madelene interrupts.

"How fond? Getting her pregnant fond? Lying to her fond? How fond, Mr. Big Shot? How fond? Tell me!" Tyreer's composure was unbelievable.

"Fond enough to ask her to marry me, ma'am."

"Marry you? Marry you? This girl don't know nothing about being a man's wife. She doesn't know that a man of your status and caliber could run over her, misuse her and abuse her and leave her for dead. She is too young to be married."

"But Mom you have always told me that when I finish college and find a job, then I could think about marriage…that you wanted me to be able to take care of myself in case something happened. I have done that. I won't be working right away because Tyreer has made sure that I can begin my graduate studies free of charge. Isn't that wonderful"?

"Yeah, it's wonderful alright. Especially when you find out that you will owe him the rest of your life. You will have to do what he says do because of what he has done for you. Your life will not be your own." (It never has been so what's the difference now.)

"Pardon me for interrupting," Tyreer chimed in. "But I have no intention of harming your daughter in anyway. I was raised a Christian man and I believe that God would not continue to bless me if I did anything to her."

"He's right you know, Madelene," Mother Niece spoke. "You and I both know that we were raised in the adoration of the Lord. You attended Church School and Sunday Service just like I did. Pastor Wright taught us all how to be Christian men and women. Although my son was not with me, he was with his father who was a Bishop and raised him to be the fine young man he is today. Madelene, you must give these young folks a chance to be happy. If it is a mistake, it's their mistake. But I believe that this is meant to be and all my son wants is your blessing." There was a long pause and finally she responded.

I Think She Said Yes, I Think

"I'm telling you right now, I don't have no money for a fancy wedding so if Bea and Tyrik, Terry, whatever the hell his name is can come up with a wedding out of their own pockets, then I'll think about being in attendance." I took that as a yes and jumped up to hug her.

"Don't run up on me like that. You know I don't like that touchy, feelie, sh__."

"Ok but thank you Mom. Thank you so much."

"Yes. Thank you, Mrs. Stanford, for giving me the honor to marry your daughter. I'll take good care of her for the rest of her life."

"Thank you, Madelene. You've made my son and my new daughter very happy."

"Alright, well I need to prepare for my trip. Let me know the date and time."

"I will Mom." We headed towards the front door all smiles. As I entered the car and looked at Madelene, I saw an angry face. I didn't understand what that meant until much later.

Graduation was over. I was a graduate with a Bachelor's degree in Business and Marketing. Madelene seemed proud until she saw Tyreer and his mother fretting over me and telling me how proud they were and how wonderful I was.

"How about we all go to dinner as a new blended family? You know, like a celebration dinner for Bea's new accomplishment," suggested Tyreer.

"And I am sure there are many more accomplishments to come. Right, Madelene?" Mother Niece beamed. Madelene took a moment to compose her thoughts before she opened her mouth which I felt was the best thing she could have done.

"I have raised Bea to never fail; to reach high and become someone people respect." We all looked as if we understood what she was really trying to say, but we didn't really know.

"You go ahead with your new blended family, Bea. I have some things I need to take care of at the house."

"But Mom, I want you to come, too."

"This is your day, enjoy it." And with that final remark, she left. The three of us stood there wondering what exactly her state of mind was. After dinner, Tyreer walked me to the door and kissed me good night.

"Good night, soon to be Mrs. Josephs."

"Good night, my handsome soon to be, Mr. Josephs." We both giggled at the thought. It seemed so hard to watch him drive away but it was early May and July would approach quickly. We had agreed to schedule the wedding for July 15th that way his family and what little bit of my family could all attend.

A Dream is Just a Dream

One week after just doing nothing, I had a surge of energy to get this wedding on the road. I tried to include Madelene in every aspect of the planning but she would have no parts of it. She would say since she didn't have a dime to spend on it, she should not have an opinion about it. It seemed so weird not having your Mother helping you, listening to you, and enjoying the fact that you are so happy. Without her knowing, I invited the company of Mother Niece along for most of it. She was so sweet and a good listener. I was glad she was going to be my mother-in-law. May whizzed by and it was already the middle of June. Tyreer had been interviewing, recruiting, and establishing residence for both of us so we talked by phone a lot. He had to be there on campus every day to get things rolling by the Fall Semester. The wedding was thirty days away. A couple of girlfriends helped me stuff favors and assisted me with my idea of centerpieces for the reception tables.

Tyreer gave me a budget of ten thousand dollars and the bulk of that went on the Venue. The most elegant ballroom in Seawall was the Meridian Hall. It looked like a royal palace and it was hard to book. Mother Niece had a hand in getting the place because her nephew had been general manager for over 10 years. It came complete with draped ceilings, chandeliers, crystal and pearls. All in my chosen color scheme of purple and gold. It was magnificent! They also provided the catering, open bar, and their in-house DJ. They would have done my centerpieces as well but I had created my own visions for those. Each table would have a King and Queen crown interlocked together. In the center of the crowns would be African violets and baby's breath along with the wedding favors. It turned out real nice. The cake was four tiers with a King and Queen on top. My dress was purple and gold with Afro-Centric braiding and Tyreer's tux was gold with purple accessories.

All details handled, all invitations sent, bridal party ready to go. It seemed as if all of this was a dream. It was really going to happen. I would get out of Hell and live in heaven on earth. I couldn't wait. Madelene didn't like the colors so she said she was going to wear pink. That made Mother Niece purchase a pink dress so that the mothers would be matching. Madelene agreed to let Papa walk me down the aisle because he missed graduation. He has always had bad sinus problems and on the day of my college graduation, he was having minor surgery to place a drainage tube in his sinus region. I was so glad he was going to be at the wedding.

It was now two weeks before the wedding and I had been so busy until I didn't notice that Tyreer hadn't called but once last week. I dismissed it as him being overwhelmed with so many things to do. But now it was Wednesday of the following week and I hadn't heard a word. I called Mother Niece and she said she hadn't heard from him either. She thought it was because he was tired and exhausted and with what energy he had left, he was talking to me. I prayed immediately that everything was alright. I tried over and over to reach him by his office phone with no luck. He had found a home for us but phone services weren't hooked up yet. I didn't want to panic but I knew something was wrong. Later that night after tossing and turning, I begged the Lord to let nothing harm my future husband. I finally drifted off to sleep while still on my knees. When I arose, I noticed it was seven in the morning. I stood up and headed towards the kitchen. As I was passing by Madelene's room, she sat straight up in her bed like a dead body arising from a casket.

"If that asshole says he wants to postpone this wedding, you tell him that you are getting married on that day or not at all!" Her trancelike state ended and she laid back down in the bed and began to snore.

I stood there thinking how strange that was for her to say something like that. Maybe she was having a dream and was only partially awake. Nevertheless,

I had to do something to ease my troubled mind. I started reading poetry but I would pause and daydream about being married to the perfect guy for me. We had so much in common. God, intelligence, success, and future parenting (we both wanted two kids— a boy and a girl). It was going to be the best rest of my life ever.

Not Again

The phone startled me out of my daydream as I came back and refocused.

"Hello?"

"Bea, it's me."

"Tyreer! Oh my God! Are you alright? Where have you been? I've been trying to reach you. I thought something bad happened to you."

"No, I'm fine. Bea, we need to talk."

"About what? Don't tell me you don't want to wear that tux. It's too late to switch it now or that…"

"Bea, listen to me. We need to talk in person. I am at the corner store from your house and I will be there to pick you up in about five minutes."

"Five minutes! I just got out of bed!"

"Just throw on a robe. I'm on my way." He sounded stressed. What was all this about? I walked quietly past my room to hers. I threw on my robe and tipped out the front door. Tyreer had already parked in front of the house. I opened the door on the passenger's side and got in.

"What on earth is going on, Tyreer?"

"Bea, there's not going to be a wedding unless you elope with me right now."

"Man, have you lost your mind? After all the planning I've done and all the money you've spent."

"I don't care about the money. All I care about is you."

"Ok. So, why are you doing this? ANSWER ME! WHY ARE YOU DOING THIS?!!!

"Ok. Somehow your mother found out where I worked on campus."

"What?"

"Listen to me. She is angry because she feels that I am taking you away from her and you belong to her and her alone. Bea, she walked into my office with a gun! She said that if I didn't call off this wedding, she would shoot you, me, and my Mom. So, we do not have any time to waste. Go get your purse and we are getting out of here. I can't let anything happen to you or my Mom."

"I can't believe this! I just can't believe this!"

"Bea go! Go now, hurry!" My mind was spinning around as I headed toward the door. By the time I reached the knob, there was Madelene standing on the other side of it with a 12-gauge shotgun. It used to belong to Papa.

"Just where do you think you're going?"

"Mother put the gun down. I was coming inside to let you know that Tyreer was here to take me to breakfast. I was going in the house to get dressed."

"What are you doing out here in front of God and everybody half-dressed anyway? He has spoiled you and made you nasty and unfit for the Kingdom of God. He has spoiled my innocent baby and for that he will pay!" She points the rifle toward Tyreer who had opened the car door to approach her.

"Tyreer, No! Don't! Please!! Go back!" But he kept walking toward Madelene. I shut my eyes tight when I heard her pull the trigger. Tyree was on the sidewalk holding onto his right leg. Blood was pouring out of the gunshot wound.

"Mom, call the operator and get an ambulance here quick, please."

"I ain't doing a damn thing. He's not gone die!" She went in the house and locked the door.

I ran next door and used the phone to get an ambulance to our address quickly. Police also arrived. While Tyreer was being transported to the hospital, I told the police what happened in detail and they wanted to question my Mother. As much as I didn't want to, I gave them the key to the house and they entered addressing who they were and calling her name.

"Mrs. Stanford, Police. Please show yourself visible with your hands up. I stayed with Tyreer and before I entered the ambulance, I saw them take her handcuffed to the patrol car. They informed me that she would be down at the station for questioning. I told them as soon as I knew the overall condition of Tyreer, I would come down to the station.

On the way to the hospital, I called Mother Niece and told her what happened. She began to sob uncontrollably.

"I told him not to do it, I told him not to. I told him not to go to your Mother's house because she is violent and obsessed with you. She will hurt or harm anyone who tries to take you away from her. Tyreer seemed to think that his prayers and faith would soften her heart and everything would be alright and for me not to worry. But she found him. She found him on his job and threatened him. Oh Lord, please don't let him die. Please Jesus, don't let him die!"

"Mother Niece, I am so sorry. He will be alright. I know he will."

"As soon as I can get myself together, I will be there, Bea."

"I will be here; I'm not leaving his side."

This Is Surreal

The medical staff rushed him off to the operating room to remove the bullet from his leg. It had made a hole passing through on the other side. It tore a muscle and hit a nerve. I was so hurt, scared and angry that she had done this to the man that I was supposed to spend the rest of my life with. I sat and waited and finally Mother Niece showed up. The look she had on her face was that of anger and disgust. I didn't know how to handle all of this.

"What did they say?" I explained that he was in surgery and the condition they told me his leg was in. By the time I finished explaining, the surgeon came to greet us and give us detailed information on his condition.

"Tyreer is going to be alright. That bullet just missed a major nerve that could have meant partial paralysis. He will have to remain hospitalized for at least a week and then physical therapy for another month. I am sorry but it looks as if he will not be able to place a lot of pressure on that leg for some time. I will order a walker and a motorized scooter when it is time for his dismissal."

At the same time, we both asked, "Can we see him!"

"He is still in recovery. I will have a nurse inform the two of you when he will be conscious enough to see you." With that, he walked away.

The look of anger had left Mother Niece's face and had been replaced with tears. Our tears flowed non-stop as we hugged one another. After a few moments, silence was the order of the atmosphere. It seemed as if time stood still as I kept reliving the horrible sound of the gunshot, the anger and demonic spirit that rest upon Madelene's face as she pulled the trigger. I think when I fell over Tyreer as she released the trigger, she intended to shoot me, too. What was wrong with her? How could anyone be so mean and hateful to consistently ruin my life?

The nurses' desk called me over and said I had an important phone call. It was at that very moment that I remembered I told the police I would be down to the police station once I knew Tyreer's status. I forgot all about going.

"Hello? This is she. I understand. I will as soon as I can but I need to speak to my fiancé as soon as he awakens. I will be at least another half hour. Yes sir, I understand. Thank you." They wanted me to come down as soon as possible to give a statement and to take my Mother home. She was not going to be charged with anything because she told them it was self-defense—that Tyreer was walking toward her so she panicked and pulled the trigger. Boy! Had she twisted that story up to no end. He was walking toward her to talk to her and to convince her to put the gun down. He had nothing, absolutely nothing, to defend himself or to hurt her with. She was not in a state of panic but in a fit of rage.

"Ms. Faye and Mrs. Niece?"

I snapped out of my phone call disgust and answered, "Here we are."

Love Is

Mother Niece had already started down the hallway to Tyreer's room. We slowly opened the door and moved quietly toward the side of the bed. His leg was in an elevated sling and it looked as if he was still in a lot of pain. Mother Niece went first.

"Son, you are going to be alright. I've already talked to God about it. The doctor said that you will be walking with assistance for a while but he is expecting a full recovery."

"Thanks for that bit of good news, Mom. But right now, I don't feel like things are so promising."

"I know baby, but they are. He promised me that they are."

I was sitting in the opposite corner of the room not knowing how to approach him or what to say. The way he had his neck turned, he couldn't see that I was in the room. I remained still and quiet.

"Where is Bea?" Mother Niece looked over in the corner and I quickly placed my finger over my lips to let her know I didn't want him to know I was there.

"She had to answer a phone call concerning the incident. She will be in shortly." He dozed off for about ten minutes.

"Bea, why didn't you want me to tell him that you were here?"

"Because…it is because of me that he is lying there with restricted movement for who knows how long. I can't face him. He must hate me."

"Bea, despite what happened today, I know my son loves you and he proved that very thing today. He took a chance on taking you out of a dangerous situation at the risk of losing his own life. That my dear, is real love."

"I just wanted to see him before I pick up my Mother from the station."

"So, they are not holding her?"

"No, they are not. And I am not holding Tyreer to his proposal either. Here, take the ring and give it back to him. Would you please?"

"Bea, what are you saying?"

"I am saying that just like he loves me enough to risk his life for me, I love him enough for him to never risk it again."

"But Bea."

"Let him know that I love him with all of my heart but I will never put his life in danger again. And with Madelene still alive, he is in danger. This is my loving sacrifice."

"But don't you think he should hear all of this from you?"

"It's too much for me to tell him right now and too much for him to hear. I am so sorry Mother Niece. I love you both so much but I just can't take the chance of losing him again. I'm so sorry. I'm so deeply sorry."

I ran out thinking about how Madelene had won, again. But this time it didn't matter as much that she had won as much as it mattered that Tyreer was still alive. The defeat was weighing heavy on me but there was nothing I could do about it but stay out of his life. It looked as if my life was pre-destined for misery and loneliness. Is this what God had planned for me? At the time, I really didn't know.

Now What

From that day on, I slowly but surely started to develop a resentment for my Mother. I asked God to help me not to feel that way about her. I had no idea how long that journey would take. Once at the station, they released her into my custody and told me that she was scheduled for a psychological evaluation on the following Tuesday. When I asked why she had to undergo this evaluation, they told me that she had changed her story a couple of times. At one point, she said, "I pulled the trigger and shot him". Another story was "He grabbed the gun from her hand to shoot me." (When the enemy has your brain, he has everything.) On Tuesday, I took Mom to the doctor's office for her evaluation.

"I'm not crazy and you are not going to make me think I'm crazy!"

"Mom, nobody said you were crazy. I think they want you to see the doctor to make sure you can recall in detail what happened that day you pulled the gun on Tyreer and shot him in the leg."

"Ty what? Ty who?"

"Tyreer, Mom. The man I was going to marry?"

"Ain't nobody getting married that I know of." I felt like telling her you've got that right!

They called her back to the examination room. She was asked all types of questions. At least seven times, she answered the same question differently. Once we were home, she seemed distant, quiet. I wish I could say at this point I was worried but I wasn't. I was enjoying the peace.

The next day, I went job hunting and browsing around the few shops we had downtown. I began to cry when I passed Lane's Bridal where I had to return my dress. I just could not see ever getting married at all.

Somehow, Mama continued to make it to her job as a domestic every day. Therefore, I was convinced that she would be alright and back to her old self in no time. I also realized that I should enjoy this mood while it lasted. We managed to have some nice conversations as I listened to stories about how hard it was for her coming up. Selfishly I thought, you think you had it hard? I could not believe how nice she had become.

Finally, they called with the results of her examination. She had entered early dementia and it was causing loss of her short-term memory. I was told to pay close attention to her because she might forget where she put things or become confused about her location. For the most part, she was handling everything very well and I was thankful for the calm spirit.

Tyreer kept calling me and I kept right on not answering. I waited at least three months when I knew he had settled in before I attempted to explain myself to him. I called his mother and asked for his telephone number but she was a little reluctant to give it to me.

"I am not sure he wants to talk to you, Bea."

"I know and I deserve that but I have to try."

"Why do you feel like you have to try now when you refused to try earlier?"

"I don't exactly know how to explain it. Perhaps, I thought my feelings for him would go away but they haven't. Yet, I know we can never be together because of my Mother."

"Bea, you are going to have to get rid of the fear of Madelene. You will never be happy or have a life of your own if you don't."

"I am sure you are right but maybe that's my destiny to be unhappy."

"Why would you think that God would want you unhappy? He is just not that kind of God."

"Like I said, I don't know but I want to talk to him. So, may I please have his number?"

"Alright dear, but don't blame me if he is less than cordial. You really hurt him."

"I know." I wrote down the number and stared at it until I mustered up the courage to dial.

"Student Recruitment Services, Tyreer Josephs speaking."

"Tyreer?"

"Bea?"

"Yes, it's me." There was the longest pause that seemed like forever. He finally spoke.

"Why did you leave me like you did? I thought you loved me enough to stick by my side no matter what. You were going to be my wife for God's sake! When I came to myself and saw your ring, I died a different kind of death. One I don't want to experience again!"

"I understand, but don't you see I had to do it for your safety?"

"For my safety or yours, Bea?" I remained silent.

"Look, I have several student events I must attend today. I appreciate your phone call and I hope things work out well for you and your Mom." He hung up. From that moment on, I decided that I would develop a tough skin as far as Madelene was concerned. I really didn't know how I was going to go about it because I was so afraid of her. Then, I remembered a scripture that I learned in BTU as a young girl: *'Greater is He that is in me than he that is in the world.'* Come on Jesus, show me Your greatness.

Chapter Ten
THE NEXT CHAPTER

Finally, I was employed by at a small PR firm where I felt there was potential to grow. Of course, Madelene, when she was really being Madelene, thought it was a dead-end job because I wasn't a schoolteacher. All and all, I suppose it could be worse. Not really knowing how Madelene would make it on her own, I made myself content with being at home, going to work and to church. The memory loss had its ups and downs. When it was down, she was down, subdued, and quiet; and drinking at least two cans of beer made her almost lethargic. Supposedly, it was a low dose of valium that made her so peaceful but in my heart of hearts, I knew her mind was slipping away.

Who Is That

One day, this extremely handsome guy came to the firm to discuss hiring us for his marketing project. He was a t-shirt print designer and wanted to really push his product. There was only one other person that dealt with marketing besides me. Her name was Tragedee, (pronounced Tragedy); what a name! None the less, she was on maternity leave, so I automatically inherited the project.

The gentleman's name was Dino Maze. Dino, like the dinosaur, and built…A-Mazing! He was from Panama, yet, a citizen of the US for over twenty-five years. He looked at least six years older than me and that was attractive. I was mature for my age, so guys in my age range didn't really click for me. I set up a meeting with him for the following day and I put my imagination to work for his project. I was smiling the rest of the day just at the thought of how he constantly smiled at me. I worked a little later than usual and told the boss I would lock up. I wanted to be well prepared for tomorrow's presentation. Normally, I leave at five but it was already going on six-thirty. I grabbed my portfolio and headed out the door. Just as I turned the key in the lock and turned around, there was Dino walking towards me. I promise he looked like a Greek God. Cold black hair of a straight texture, bronze skin, sultry grey eyes and smooth just-the-right-size lips! Lord, have mercy on me!!

"Woah! You startled me!"

"Forgive me, that was not my intention. I saw a light on, so I wanted to come back and share something with you about my project. I know you're the expert in all of this but I wanted to share another one of my ideas with you."

"Unfortunately, we are closed until tomorrow at nine."

"I am aware of that now. I rode around trying to decide if I was going to share the idea with you or not and I guess I must have waited too late."

"I guess so." His eyes twinkled like I used to imagine that Santa Claus' eyes twinkled.

"Unless you'd be willing to spare an hour of your time over coffee this evening?"

"I wouldn't mind if it weren't so late. I have a mother at home that can't been left alone without monitoring for extended periods of time once she leaves her job around three. I am usually there with her by five. Thanks for the invitation though. Would you like for me to hold off on my presentation in case you would like to incorporate yours?"

"Honestly, I have set a deadline but I don't want to rush your work either. Tell you what, what I'd like to share will not take more than an hour. How about we meet for coffee about eight? I will be done by the time you need to arrive at work. Since your presentation for the project is not until two in the afternoon, that will give you time to include the idea if you think it will work. What do you think?"

"That's something I can do. I will meet you at Denny's at eight am then?"

"Sounds terrific, see you then." He walked me to my car like Tyreer used to do and bid me goodnight. I had to tell myself all the way home, do not focus on the face and the body, focus on the heart, and of course, the work.

By now it was close to seven pm and I was starving. Mom had already said we would be having left over chicken and rice but I did not feel chicken and rice-cy. I was feeling more like a Bigger Burger. I felt strong and powerful after the conversation with Dino. I felt that I could win him and keep him as a customer. Earlier, I had called Madelene to tell her that I would be working late. Her memory was on a down and she responded with a sweet, "That's fine. I am ok." I stopped by Bigger Burger and then I headed home. When I arrived home and opened the door, it looked like a tornado had hit the living room. She was on the warpath. She was throwing things and cussing and fussing to the top of her voice.

"What's the matter?"

"What do you mean, what's the matter!? You're the matter! You know that I am hungry and I don't have anything to eat. I've been waiting on you to take me to get something to eat. Then, you come walking in here with a Bigger Burger bag in your hand asking me what's the matter!!"

"Mom, calm down. You told me when I called you earlier that we were having left over chicken and rice for supper. I told you I was working late and you said, 'It's ok I'll be fine'. I stopped to get something to eat because I knew you had already eaten and put the food away. Now, you are angry at me and I don't really understand why." Madelene was only sixty-four years old but in that moment, her face sunk to an eighty-year-old sad woman who had behaved like a spoiled child.

"I did tell you about the chicken and rice, didn't I?"

"Yes, ma'am, you did." She sat down in her favorite chair and lit a cigarette.

"You know, I think that medicine the doctor gave me is making me forget things. I'm not taking any more of that stuff."

"I'm not sure you should stop taking it without asking the doctor." (Besides, I love the medicated you.)

"I'm not asking him a damn thing. I know it's making me sick and I'm not taking it!"

"Ok, if you say so. Would you like for me to heat up the chicken and rice for you?"

"No, I'll get me a glass of water and go on to bed since you didn't think to bring me a Bigger Burger." I can't believe she seemed to understand why I didn't bring her a burger one minute, and the next minute she didn't understand.

"Here Mom, you can have this one. I can eat the chicken and rice." She smiled and took my Bigger Burger. Man, I wanted that.

I've Got This

I was up at six and out the door by seven-thirty. I explained to Mom that I had an early business meeting and I would be home at the regular time today. Once again, she said she understood and she would be fine until I came home. I arrived at Denny's about seven forty-five and Dino was already there. He exited his Mercedes Coupe and opened my door for me. Once inside, we discussed his idea. It was corny and I didn't know how to tell him that so, I was going to show him. I would place his idea inside my presentation and show it to him. Then, I would show him my presentation minus his idea.

"Let's take a look at both of the finished promotions side by side in our meeting this afternoon, shall we?"

"Sure, that would be great. Are you going to have enough time to do all of that by two?"

"But of course, Mr. Maze, especially if I stop enjoying the company so much and get to work."

"I am enjoying the company as well. But you're right, it's almost nine and I will no longer detain you."

"Thank you, so much." I smiled.

As we parted ways, I immediately began to revamp my presentation inside of my head. Once inside my office, I was able to splice and paste to include Dino's idea. I hoped, with all that was in me, that he would recognize his idea was not beneficial to the overall project. A couple of calls came in for possible projects, so I set appointments. The morning seemed to drag on for days. I was anxious to show Mr. A- Mazing my work. I felt I had a point to prove: I know what I am doing.

Mr. Maze was prompt, in fact, he arrived ten minutes early.

"Let's see what you have Ms. Faye. It is Ms. isn't it?"

"Yes, it is." We spent a few moments in a deep mutual smile.

Over the next fifteen minutes, I was a regular show off. The promo was complete with bells and whistles, color, and class. He was impressed. Then I showed him the same presentation with his idea included. He was not impressed with that one. I had won him over and he agreed to let our firm handle his account. I went ahead and discussed target dates and how to push the brand and still meet the deadline he was anticipating.

On his way out, he asks if perhaps we could have dinner next time. I told him I would let him know. Dinner was going to be tricky especially when I never knew if Madelene was going to be up or down. I know I would not mind spending some "social" time with Mr. A-Mazing, I just could not figure out when. Here I was a graduate, working a decent job, yet living with my Mother. I know she is not going to want to hear it, but I need to move out. I need my own space. I need to invite Dino over.

The Maze account was wrapped up and Dino's sales were flying off the charts. He was well pleased with my work and so was my boss. I was offered the position of Director of Marketing and I was super excited. I would have the opportunity to hire a creative assistant which would take some of the heaviest loads off me. Not to mention that the position would raise my salary an extra ten thousand dollars a year. Thank You, Lord! Most of all, this meant I could move out and have my own living space. Things were looking up.

The Lord Will Make A Way Somehow

One Friday evening, I arrived home to find Madelene sitting quietly staring at the television set. It was not turned on. When I asked if she would like for me to turn it on, she simply said, "No." I knew she had to be in deep thought but I had not a clue as to what it could be about. I quietly moved around, unwinding, and making sure food was available for her to eat. She had bought two chicken meals from Kentucky and they were sitting on the cabinet.

"Bea, I bought some chicken for supper; all thighs."

"Thanks. Why haven't you eaten yet?"

"I thought I was hungry but my hunger went away." I moved from the kitchen to the living room and sat on the loveseat adjacent to her chair.

"Is there something wrong?"

"I no longer have a job."

"What happened?"

"Mr. and Mrs. Redford are moving to Florida. He is retiring from the law firm and they want to spend the rest of their days relaxing on the beach. So, they are retiring me along with them. I will get six months' pay but after that I won't have nothing!"

"Of course, you will Mama. Remember how you've always taught me that the Lord will make a way somehow?"

"Yeah, I taught you that."

"Then, it is time to believe that what you taught me is true for you, too. I will help you; you will be alright."

"I suppose you are right. Besides, with you staying here at the house you can help me out on the utilities if need be." Wow, what horrible timing to talk about moving out.

"Of course, I will help you especially now that I have been promoted to Director of Marketing for the firm. My salary will increase considerably and you will not have to worry about your bills falling behind."

"Really? Well, that's good Bea. I knew the Lord would eventually bless me for saving your life. If it hadn't been for me, you would have been dead by now and I wouldn't have had any help." I refused to comment.

I went back to the kitchen and heated up the meals in the oven. I brought hers to her while I sat in the kitchen thinking. I was washing the plates and cleaning up the kitchen when it occurred to me that Madelene would be sixty-five in about three months. I would help her apply for social security and that would be some additional income that she would be able to live off with or without me. I just pray that the Redford's took social security out of her check. Since she worked for a private household, I didn't know whether they did that or not. I was determined to find out.

The next day while on a break, I called Mrs. Redford. She assured me that social security had been taken out for all the twenty years Madelene worked for them. I was so grateful. I would set up an appointment and start the process. I took care of all her finances anyway and had access to her social and whatever else I needed including yearly salary statements if they needed them.

The Redford's would be moving to Florida in about a week. Friday of that same week would be her last day. They were truly kind to her, well to us, over the years. This is the firm that gave me the full two-year scholarship to SJC. They gave her an envelope with two hundred dollars in it that day. They called it a "Thank You" bonus. Two hundred dollars all at once was a lot of money back then considering she had to work a whole month to make two hundred dollars. She seemed happy, yet sad. Here was a woman who had worked as a domestic since age eleven. And now for the first time in fifty-four years, she was going to be without work. I began to have mixed emotions about moving out. Yet, I knew I had to do what was best for me. I had been under her rule of thumb long enough and it was time for me to start living a life of my own. In about a month, Mom's first social security check arrived.

Making It On My Own

Dino and I had moved a little closer to being an item, but no labels just yet. In between my work assignments and monitoring Mom, we'd have a lunch date here and there. Mainly, we communicated by phone. We would have wee-hour conversations after she had fallen off into a deep sleep. I learned a lot about his childhood in Panama and how his parents struggled as immigrants once they arrived in the US. They finally became entrepreneurs by owning their own grocery market. They have passed on to Heaven now but his parents instilled in him a work ethic that has governed his entire life. His t-shirt design business was only one of his projects. He also designed billboards and posters for major companies. He informed me that whenever I saw the initials DM on any print type design, it was more than likely his logo. I was impressed that he had done so well and was still humble about it.

One afternoon, I left work early to look for an apartment. I invited Dino to come along. Moving to an area that was not too far from work or Mom was not going to be a simple task. There was lots of new construction going on in town but most of it was on the far west side. The firm and my Mom's house were North Central. All the apartments in that area were rather shabby and the residents didn't seem to be professional. We drove over to the west side just to check things out.

Dino lived in The Higher Heights Condominiums and invited me in to see his place. Wow! I would have loved to be able to live in a place like that. It had vaulted ceilings, chandeliers, marble and Italian tile and his décor was amazing. I loved it; just couldn't afford it at the tune of two thousand-five hundred dollars a month. He was a good tour guide and host. He shared stories behind his success and his paintings. After about an hour, we drove around looking at the new apartment buildings that were going up. Although I inquired, I wasn't sure if I wanted to live this far away. A one bedroom was eight hundred dollars a month, which was quite a bit of change back then. I decided to see if we could find something in that same price range on my side of town.

We drove back over and covered just about every complex visible. I didn't like any of them. They all looked rather run down and creepy. Like maybe drug runners lived there. I was looking for something a little more professional. Dino drove me back to my car at the firm and we said our goodbyes vowing to talk later that night. Frustration came over me. My regular feeling of hopelessness surrounded me. It was almost closing time at the firm, so I went inside to see if I had any important messages. Nothing major.

As I drove off headed toward the house, I remembered an invoice I had to drop off at the Liston Feed Company, which was on the way. Good thing it was still on the back seat of my car. After dropping off the invoice, traffic had backed up on the main street and I did not feel like waiting. Taking a side street by the Feed Co., I noticed a quaint little house with a For Lease sign in the yard. I stopped in front to write down the number on the sign when I saw an older lady coming out the front door. She started to approach my car.

"Hello, are you interested in leasing a property?"

"Actually, I'm not sure. Are you the realtor?"

"No. I'm the owner, Stella Ward. My son thinks I have gotten too old to live by myself, so I am leasing the property and moving to Cashew with he and his family. Would you care to see it?"

"Sure, why not." I followed her up the sidewalk to a well-manicured lawn that had sunflowers and daisies blooming in the flower beds. She unlocked the door and invited me inside. It was simply beautiful. It was fully furnished with an early American feel. Spic and Span and it smelled like baked cookies. It was a two-bedroom, two-bath home with so much character. As we walked and talked while I inspected things, she told me how she and her late husband built this cute little place with their bare hands. Before I knew it, we were having coffee and I was spilling my guts to her about why I felt I needed to move. She became sad at the thought of my Mother not loving me. She assured me that she loved me but perhaps she didn't know how to show it.

"Sometimes people don't know how to show love because love was never shown to them." This indeed was a wise woman.

"Okay, so how much are you asking per month?"

"My son said I should lease it for nine hundred dollars per month. But I think that's too much for you, dear. For you, I will lease it for seven hundred dollars per month. I have a good feeling about you, a spiritual feeling and I know you will take good care of my little treasure."

"I most certainly will. I've been gone most of the afternoon looking at apartments, the new ones on the west side and the older ones on this side of town. I really wanted something over here because it would be closer to my job as well as my Mom."

"I am leaving for Cashew in the morning to move some of those boxes to my son's house. I will be there at least a week. Would you be ready to move in and sign the lease by then?"

"I don't see why not. Since it is fully furnished and I love the décor, all I have to do is move in my clothes and personals."

"Very well then dear, we will meet here on next Saturday at about ten am. Is that good for you?"

"Yes, ma'am. That is perfect. I'll see you then." I saw myself out but waited until she locked the door and got in her car to leave. Ms. Ward had shared with me that she was 79 years old. Yet, she was so alert and healthy. She was mentally sharp and had a beautiful smile that looked as if she still had all her original teeth. She was so sweet and nice. I was going to enjoy living in this cute little house. *'Oh Lord, help me choose the right time to tell Madelene!'*

When Will It Be The Right Time

Once at home, it was obvious that this was not the right time, again. Madelene had taken every dish out of her China cabinet and was washing them. That might not have been so bad except she was fussing about no one else is going to eat from these dishes. Now, I know for a fact we very seldom had company. She has always said that those dishes were kept for when company came. So, I am wondering did someone come over while I was at work or what?

"Mom, why are washing the good china?"

"Because I am not going to let anybody eat from these dishes if I haven't eaten from them myself."

"Who is trying to eat from them?"

"There were some people here earlier that I didn't know and they came straight to my china cabinet. I told them they could not eat off these plates but they just kept trying to set the table so they could eat." I looked around. I saw no food and no sign of a table setting.

"Mom, did you take your medicine today?" Everything became quiet, a cold still quiet, then she spoke.

"I can't find them." She started crying.

"It's ok, I will help you find them Mom, don't worry." I begin to cry, too. Something was wrong and neither of us knew exactly what. The pill box was sitting where it always sat with that day's pill unremoved. I gave it to her and sat her down with a glass of water. Once it kicked in, she was still and quiet. I finished drying the dishes, placing them back in the cabinet while she watched TV. My heart was troubled, what was wrong with her?

She's Still Holding On

The following Monday, I made an appointment with her Primary Care doctor and explained to him the episode I had witnessed. He scheduled her for some tests on Thursday. A half day was all I worked that day so I could take her to the doctor. They ran all types of tests that kept us there until six o'clock. We were told to come back on Tuesday for the results. What a dilemma. I was to meet Ms. Ward on Saturday to sign the lease for the house and there has not been a good time to tell Mama I was moving out. I contacted Ms. Ward by phone to inform her that I would not be able to sign the lease on Saturday. I further explained what happened and I didn't feel comfortable moving out before the test results came back. She said she understood and she would hold the place if she could, but her son was more anxious than she to have someone in there. I apologized and thanked her for considering holding it for me and that I would contact her as soon as possible. Lord, I hope it's still available when Mama gets better.

When Tuesday came, the doctor sat both of us down to explain that Mama was having some bouts with dementia.

Although she had just reached 65, the onset could have been brought on by some sort of stress. It is not uncommon and it certainly isn't fatal. He questioned her about any major changes in her life. She confessed that not having a job anymore made her feel useless. He suggested that she develop a hobby. I interjected that fishing had been her hobby for years. With that information, he insisted that she get back to fishing. It would clear her head and help her get back to her old self again. He prescribed Razadyne, an approved medication for mild to moderate stages of dementia. We both felt better informed when we left the office that day.

Back at home, I devised a plan for her to remember to take her pill. She drank two cups of coffee every morning, so I placed her pill box right by her coffee cup. She never forgot to take them again. I felt guilty about moving out now so I contacted Ms. Ward and told her I wouldn't be able to lease the place after all. With Mom's health scare, it was better if I stuck around a little longer. Ms. Ward was disappointed because now she had to find someone that she felt would really take care of the place all over again. With all the sweetness that she had, she was kind enough to say she understood. That made me feel not as guilty. There were new demands being placed on me by the new position and some of it included travel. Knowing how Madelene felt about me being out of her reach, she was back to her old controlling self and gave me a hard time whenever I had to leave town.

"I believe you are lying. I know you are not going out of town because of your job, you are going to meet some man so you can hoe around like your Mama!" I would try and assure her that it was work related and that I had to go. Most of the time, I was only gone overnight and I would be back in town before noon the next day. And as far as meeting a man was concerned, Dino and I rarely talked anymore because I was so swamped at work and he was trying to sell his business in Atlanta. Madelene had nerve enough to call my boss,

Mr. Ross, and tell him to stop sending me out of town to meet up with one of his buddies that would pay me to sleep with him. He told her that he could justify every trip but he wasn't going to. Mr. Ross told her that he ran a business not a brothel and he would sue her for libel if she continued to harass his business ethics.

"If you do not trust your own daughter to meet the requirements of this job, then perhaps she should look for another one." With that, she shut up about me traveling. She knew that I paid every bill and she kept her two-hundred-and-ten-dollar social security check all to herself, no questions asked.

Taking A Stand

My life was back to being humdrum as usual. Work, home, church. No social life or special someone. Every time it looked as if my life was turning out to be something good, evil was waiting on the other side. I know I shouldn't refer to my own Mother as evil, I just didn't know how else to describe it. Mr. Ross was pleased at how I ran the Marketing Department so he chose me to be the firm's representative at a huge PR Conference in Atlanta.

"Bea, you are one of the best directors I have ever had. No one is more deserving than you to represent this firm at the National Conference."

"Thank you so much, Mr. Ross. I will be sure and put us on the map at the Conference. How long is the event?"

"It's one week and all your expenses, including accommodations, air travel and registration fees are taken care of. There is a one-thousand-dollar bonus involved that you may use however you like." By this time, I was in tears. I felt so honored and special.

"Bea, please don't cry. You work so hard and you deserve some enjoyment for your hard labor. The most important part of the Conference will be in the middle of the week on Wednesday. You do not, I repeat, do not have to attend until then. Your representation and presentation will be done on that day and you would have completed the task of being there."

"But what will I do the remainder of the week? What will I do Monday, Tuesday, Thursday, Friday, and Saturday?"

"Whatever you wish! Go shopping. Enjoy the historic sights, whatever you want. Bea, I am sending you on a well-deserved vacation! It's not necessary that you attend this Conference at all. In all my years of business, I may have gone once and that was because it was in Vegas! I had a great time. That's what I want for you, Bea, a great time. A chance to get away from Seawall and that mother of yours. I don't mean to be rude or try and run your life but she is still controlling you like a child." I was stunned at his correct analogy and description of my life. I just didn't know whether to agree or disagree, so I just said thank you.

Mr. Ross didn't give me much time to prepare Madelene for my departure and the length of my stay. I received the news on a Thursday and my flight was leaving out on Sunday. I had to have everything in order before I told her I was going to be gone for a week. Since her retirement from the work force, sometimes Mama felt like cooking and sometimes, she did not. The corner market sold prepared meals that you could cook in the oven for about thirty minutes and they were tasty. I had brought a couple of them home before for her to try. She favored the roast beef and the baked chicken. Making a list, I placed prepared meals at the top. I would stop by the market and get enough for all week. She rarely ate breakfast, only coffee. At lunch, she preferred to snack on leftovers, so the prepared meals were for supper.

Next, was to pay Mama Ethelene (Ethel) a visit. This was her old fishing buddy from way back when, before Naylor. I stopped by Mama Ethel's house during my lunch break and asked her if she could help me out with Madelene while I was away. She had the sweetest personality and always made me laugh.

"Don't you worry now, Bea. I'll keep the old coot occupied." We both laughed. She promised me she would cook up a couple of fishing trips because she'd just bought a new truck; a truck that hadn't been to the best fishing spots yet. That was number two on my list.

Number three was Papa. I had to convince him to drive by the house at least three times a week and see if anything looked out of order. If he never saw her come out of the house or if he noticed that her car hadn't moved in a couple of days, call the police. Papa had no problem with my request. As mean as she had been to him, he still loved her.

With everything checked off the list, it was time to face the music. Time to tell Madelene that I would be gone for a week but there would be food and fishing and fellowship. I would promise to call every day that I was away to make sure things were going alright. I walked in with confidence and she was sitting at the dining room table staring at a bunch of papers with a cigarette in one hand and her chin in the other. She noticed I had a big grocery bag and became alert and curious.

"What's all that?"

"I thought it might be nice if you didn't have to cook every day, so I bought some of those prepared meals you like from the market."

"I don't know why you bought so many. I'm not going to eat those things every day. If I don't feel like cooking, you're going to have to cook! You think just because you have a little old piece of a job that you can come in this house and mistreat me? No, ma'am, I'm not having it. I didn't raise you to be trifling and lazy. Your ass is going to get in that kitchen and cook!"

"Honestly, I can't get in the kitchen and cook if I am not here."

"What do you mean if you are not here? Where do you think you're going?" I convinced myself that today was the day that I would show no fear. Today was the day that I would stand up for myself, for my sanity, for my life.

"Mr. Ross is sending me on a business trip to Atlanta. I'll be gone a week starting this Sunday. I will return on the following Sunday. I bought the meals so you wouldn't have to cook so much while I am away. Mama Ethelene wants to take you fishing, just to get out of the house. You haven't been out much since you retired."

"Why you sneaky conniving heifer! Who is he?? Got dammit who is he? I said!"

"What? Who is who??"

"Don't play dumb with me. Who is the man you are going to lay up with for a whole week? You know what I am talking about!"

"There is no man, Mama. It's work. It is a business trip, that's all."

"That is not all and I know it. You walk around here like you think you are better than me just because you have a college degree when it was me who helped you get it. I scrubbed floors on my hands and knees for you to get that degree and here I am by myself and you are so ready to leave me."

"Lord! It's just a week. Get over it!"

She raised her left hand slightly coiled to mar my face with her two-inch hard-as-bricks fingernails. I reached up and grabbed her hand, her nails dug into my left arm. She scratched me down to the white flesh of my arm, it was bleeding. I grabbed her hand and pulled her pinky back as hard as I could and broke it. She screamed in pain. I didn't care. I was in pain and was grateful that it wasn't my face that was bleeding down to the flesh. I ran into my room taking the telephone with me and shut the door. I called our next door neighbor and told her that I had broken my Mom's finger to keep her from marring my face. She thought that was horrible—not that I stopped her from marring my face for life but that I had broken her finger.

"Please, if you don't mind, I will pay you gas money to take her to the emergency room so that something can be done about the broken finger". She finally agreed. I packed a few clothes for the week, grabbed my suitcase and headed toward the front door. She had wrapped the finger in an old rag and held it against a small sandwich bag of ice. When I passed by and looked at her, for the first time, I realized what IF LOOKS COULD KILL meant.

"Goodbye, Mama. See you in a week."

I hurried out the door knowing that my flight did not leave until Sunday so I booked a hotel room between the airport and Seawall for the next couple of nights. I was determined that she was not going to ruin this for me, so I refused to call the house. I lounged around and thumbed through marketing magazines and did a couple of crossword puzzles. When evening came, I walked across the street to Dairy Queen for a fast-food fix then headed back to my room. Guilt began to overwhelm me. About seven o'clock , I called Mrs. Cole, our neighbor.

"Mrs. Cole, it's Bea Faye, Madelene's daughter."

"Oh, Hello."

"I just wanted to check and see how my Mom was doing and what did they do about her finger?" She explained that the finger had been placed in a splint and she was given some pain medication.

"I just left her sleeping like a baby. She's going to be fine Bea. You go ahead with your trip. I will drop in on her and make sure that she's doing alright." She sounded totally different than she did when the incident first happened. I was this monster that broke her mother's finger and then fled the scene. This raised an eyebrow for me, why the change.

"Thank you, Mrs. Cole, I'd appreciate that. Uh, Mrs. Cole?"

"Yes?"

"I have a quick question. When I first told you, what happened you seemed terribly upset with me. Now you are telling me to go on with my business trip and everything will be fine. What changed your mind?"

"I saw your arm. When you were getting in your car to leave, I saw your arm." I breathed a sigh of relief.

Life Ain't So Bad

Mama was going to be alright and I was on my way to an all-expense paid vacation! There is a God. My flight left at seven the next morning. I became excited again. *'Lord, please let me sleep.'*

It was Sunday morning and I drove my car to the airport and parked in long term parking. Always being early has its advantages. The airport was nice and quiet. Vendors had opened and you could smell the pastries and the fresh brewed coffee. There was at least forty-five minutes before my flight arrived so I made myself comfortable while reading the JET magazine I had just purchased.

Reading was always such a good escape for me. I loved it and I absorbed myself in it. Suddenly, a gentleman sat across from me. Not really making eye contact, I kept my head in my magazine. Next thing I knew, he was sitting on the same row with me. I could feel him staring at me from the side. I will not fear! I will not fear!

Putting the magazine down, I turned to him and said, "Sir!" Then my mouth flew open in surprise. It was Dino Maze.

"Dino?? What are you doing here?"

"Oh, no how have you been? I've missed you… nothing like that huh?"

"I'm sorry. I'm just so shocked to see you. I haven't heard from you in weeks."

"Bea, I have called your house at least twice a week for the past three weeks. I wanted you to know that I was still going to do business with your firm but I had relocated to Atlanta. Your Mother would always say you were not home or that you were working late. I have a policy to not call people on their jobs unless it's an emergency because that's the same respect I need on my job. So, I kept calling your house until she started hanging up on me when she heard my voice. I just thought you were avoiding me and convinced your Mother to help out in giving me the message." I was seething with anger.

"How dare she! She never mentioned that I had received any calls at all. I never knew you called."

"Honestly, she never told you I called?"

"Never."

"In that case, I apologize for thinking what I was thinking. Since you did such a good job with my designs, I thought you were done with me."

"Funny how the mind works, isn't it? Since I never heard from you again, I felt that you had gotten all you needed from me and had become too busy to give me the time of day."

"Well will you look at us. Neither of us were correct on this one. I certainly will never be too busy to spend time with you."

"And I will never use my Mother or anyone else to avoid you because I don't want to avoid you at all."

"Good. I'm glad we've got that settled."

"By the way, Mr. Maze, where are you headed so early this morning?"

"Back to Atlanta. I was in Austin finalizing a billboard contract. Things ran over so I decided to stay an extra day. The flights out of Austin were booked so I took a small airplane shuttle here to Seawall to fly back out. And now I am so glad I did." My cheeks blushed. We sat and talked until our plane arrived. Once aboard, we had to part because he was in first class and I was in coach. There were two empty seats beside me and I was wondering who would occupy them. Everyone had boarded and the plane was in takeoff mode.

Once in the air, the flight attendant gave her spill about safety precautions and later turned off the seatbelt sign. I turned my head toward the window as we ascended into the clouds. I thought about Heaven. How beautiful it must be up there. No worries, no pain, no heartbreak. The clouds began to take on shapes, I thought I saw angels and a throne.

I was so mesmerized by the clouds that I wasn't aware that the seat next to me was now taken. A slight brush over my hand brought me back from my fantasized daydream to a real live dreamboat. Dino had given up his first-class seat to come and sit by me in coach. We looked each other in the eyes. He pulled my chin close to his lips and kissed me. I had never been kissed like that before, not even on the night I lost my virginity. We chatted a bit before he opened his laptop to complete some contracts. I took a nap. Before long, the plane landed at Hartsfield International Airport. Waiting in baggage claim, I informed him that the firm made reservations for me at the Omni Hotel adjacent to the Convention Center. He said he knew exactly where it was and that he would love to take me to dinner. I agreed and told him to give me his number and after I rested a bit, I would give him a call.

Now This Is Living

My room was immaculate! It was the business penthouse suite fit for a CEO of a Fortune 500 company. Everything was so elaborate. I was in awe. Had I really been worth all of this to Mr. Ross or was this some sort of trap? Was there a catch? I had to make myself stop believing and thinking the way Madelene taught me. I had to stop it immediately.

As I unpacked my suitcase, I realized that I had only grabbed business attire and nothing to go to dinner in. I wanted to lie down but there was no time. Surely this hotel had an in-house boutique and I had to find it pronto. Downstairs there were several shops for designer handbags, shoes, perfumes and jewelry. I didn't spot one boutique. I walked into a Tiffany's and asked the clerk if there was a boutique where I could purchase a nice cocktail dress. Okay, so grant it I didn't look like a CEO at that moment—my hair was pulled back beneath my black baseball cap and I was still wearing a tee shirt and jeans.

"Who is inquiring, may I ask?"

"I am inquiring."

"And who might you be? Who do you work for or who are you accompanying on this trip?"

"Excuse me? I find that question insulting! Why would I have to be here working for someone or sleeping with someone to purchase a cocktail dress?"

"We don't have many of your kind coming in an expensive store like this inquiring about other expensive things you probably cannot afford without the assistance of someone else's credit card."

"How dare you! Listen lady, you see this?" I pulled out my Black Diamond card with a balance of thirty thousand dollars available on it.

"And do you see this?" I pulled out my driver's license that matched the name on the credit card. She stared at both items in amazement. Everyone knows that a Black Diamond card back then could have no less than twenty thousand on it in order for it to remain active.

"Oh, I am so sorry. Ms. Faye, is it? It's just that..."

"There is no need to explain, now you see this?" I patted my behind in her face and walked out. I never felt so slighted before in a public place in my life. I was running out of time; perhaps, I would cancel dinner for tonight and go shopping tomorrow. After all I didn't come empty handed. I still had my bonus and my Black card. I knew I could find something nice on tomorrow.

I called Dino and explained why I was cancelling dinner. He sounded disappointed but understood. He was adamant about how I should have never been treated that way. He had done some store and city-wide billboard designs for Tiffany's and knew the owner of the entire franchise.

"I will be calling Ralph Pierre tomorrow and letting him know how one of the Atlanta clerks treated you. She will no longer work there! Believe me! He is an advocate of racial equality, not discrimination."

"Dino, I am not trying to cause someone to lose their job but she was really rude."

"And she is really out of there or else I will never do business with him again. He would not like that one bit. Did you happen to see her name on her tag?"

"Uh, let me see. I think it said Carolyn Cross. Yea, Carolyn Cross."

"Ok, that's' all I need. You get some rest and I will pick you up for dinner around seven tomorrow evening. Will that be okay?"

"Yes, that's fine. Goodnight, sweet Prince."

"Goodnight, my love." Okay, not going to read too much into the "goodnight, my love" statement but it would be nice if I were his love, I think.

The next day, which was Monday, was so fun and adventurous. I went to the Underground Shopping Mall and found the perfect little black dress. I hadn't really noticed that all the stress at home and at work had dropped me from a Size 12 to a Size 8. All my business suits were bought a little big because I didn't want anything tight stretching across my body when I was presenting. This was a welcomed surprise.

I was smoking hot in this dress that had a V neck and a crossover tie at the waist. I was sexy, yet classy. I found a hair salon to freshen up my braids and put them in an up do. I had a manicure and a pedicure done and took in a couple of historical sites nearby. I had been out of the room since eight o'clock that morning and it was almost three pm now. Back inside, I showered and laid out my clothes for the evening. Relaxing never felt so good. I slipped into a soft sleep and was awakened by the phone ringing.

"Hello?"

"Bea, it's me. I am running a little behind. Let us push our dinner date to eight?"

"Okay, sure that's fine, I'll see you then." I never cared to eat after six in the evening; seven was already pushing it, now eight! I don't know if I want to compete with a man and his business. When would he have quality time for me? Oh well, it's just dinner. Dino called me when he arrived in the lobby. When I stepped off the elevator, his eyes almost jumped out of his head.

"Wow, you look absolutely stunning!"

"Why thank you, sir."

"Shall we go?"

"We shall." He extended his arm out and I embraced it. Outside was a Cadillac limousine in sparkling silver. The driver opened the door as I sat inside.

"So where are we going, Mr. Maze?"

"I am taking you to the Capital Grille in Buckhead Village. I hope you like it."

"It really doesn't matter where we go, sir. As long as I'm with you, I'll like it." We kissed all the way there.

The restaurant was five stars—the food was delicious; the service was first class; and the atmosphere--delightful. I had a wonderful time.

On the way back, Dino wanted me to know where he lived. He lived in Buckhead in the Park Avenue Condos. His place blew me away. Winding staircase. Glass marble floors. I thought Tyreer's place was something, this place ran circles around his. In mild discussion about his dwellings, I managed to ask him how much the lease per month was.

"Oh, I don't lease it. I bought it. The posted cost was sixteen million dollars but I talked them down to half that amount." I am thinking to myself, eight million dollars; this dude paid eight million dollars for this place. Dang, he must have heavy pockets or maybe he does something illegal along with this design stuff. Maybe it's just a front for what he really does. BEA STOP!

"Well, it's really something."

Dino gave me the grand tour of the five-bedroom, four bath mini castle. It was something straight out of a fairytale. His master bedroom was as large as one entire side of the restaurant that we just left. Polar Bear white rug, silver headboard with embedded crystals, satin bedding, and sheets and high back silver and black chairs fit for a king. There was also an armoire that housed his television set and stereo system. And the bathroom—the bathroom was all gold and black. I had never seen or been in such a place.

"Why don't you take your shoes off Queen and relax or will you turn into a pumpkin at midnight?"

"No, but I don't want to turn into your one-night stand at midnight."

"And you won't. I am not good with for one nights only."

He dimmed the lights and slowly started to undress me with his eyes. I told him I did not want what we had in the way of friendship to be taken advantage of. He enlightened me that what he felt for me was more than friendship and that I should have known that.

"Look, I think I better go. I don't want to take things too far, too fast.

"That's fine. I will have the driver take you back to the hotel.

"You're not coming with me?"

"I will see you to the car but I have to fly out to Florida tomorrow by noon. I will be back in town on Thursday. I will get in touch with you then." He walked me to the car and said goodnight.

As we were driving, the driver says to me, "Mr. Maze must like you a lot."

"What makes you say that?"

"He never takes a young lady to his residence. He always says it's too risky. That once they find out where he lives, how important of a man he is, how rich he is, they want to take advantage of him. He must trust you." I smiled in my soul.

"I guess."

Once back at the hotel, I kept reliving the entire night. I had never been treated so royally. Tyreer was the only one who came close before Madelene shot him in the leg. Thank God, she doesn't know about Dino—she'd probably try and shoot him, too. No, I think Dino would do something to my Mama if she tried to harm him. It's best to keep them apart for as long as I can.

On Wednesday, I attended the Conference and made a pitch for our small firm with maybe a couple of bites. I see why Mr. Ross didn't come to this one often. You had to swim with the big boys or get eaten by the sharks. I received a couple of business cards from future contacts and a couple of dinner invitations but that was about it. I was tired from being on my feet all day and ready for a long hot bath and some shut eye.

The next morning was Thursday, the day Dino would be back in town. It was also the day I made up in my mind that I would spend the night with him. But he never called. Not all day nor that night. I called him on Friday morning just to make sure he was alright, but no answer. I guess Mama was right, 'all men want is to take advantage of your body. If you do not yield it to them, they are done.' Then…so am I.

My Life Must Begin

The next couple of days, I wandered around the streets of Atlanta, took a couple of guided tours and laid down a lot. Next thing I knew, it was Sunday. Time to head back to Seawall, to my Mama's house. One thing for sure, I was not going to take the chance of her harming me again. I was going to find an apartment so help me God! When it came to her, fear could no longer be a factor. All my life I had been afraid to tell her what I think, what I really want to do or who I really want to become. All I have ever done is try and make her love me and show it. What harm would a hug do every now and then? Instead, she adopted me to rule over me and teach me to be afraid not to follow her rules. I have had enough. I am almost twenty-five years old and my life must begin, no matter how much she is determined to emotionally end it! My determination to survive must be stronger. My faith must become greater than it's ever been before.

As a young adult, I had every right to live my own life. Why couldn't she trust the way she raised me? It has been a vague truth that if you forbid a child to do something, it becomes a strong desire to do it. Under normal circumstances, I might would agree. But under the roof of Madelene Faye, under the umbrella of darkness, under the shadow of fear, I would not chance disobeying her. Obeying your parents meant that your life would be long on this earth. As a child, I abided by that rule. Now as an adult, although she was older, I was in the same category with her. Adulthood. As far as I'm concerned, it is no longer a matter of obedience but of decision. A decision to take myself out of harm's way. A decision to become a whole adult. I was intelligent, gifted and blessed. Those three factors alone proved that I did not have to live my life under anyone's thumb— especially if they were capable of shooting off your leg!

Coming to the point of decision making concerning where I live and who I live with was long overdue. You only have one life to live. You must choose the right path for your life. *'Lord, let me choose right. I know that only You can guide me to the correct path. I have tried to honor her in every way that I know how. It is my inner most desire for You to be pleased Lord, so help me. Help make it through this life.'*

Chapter Eleven
All That Glitters Ain't Goal

When I arrived at the airport, I waited on my baggage and headed toward the long-term parking lot. Upon my approach, I saw Dino standing right beside my car. Who does this guy think he is after standing me up in Atlanta?

"Why are you here? What do you want?"

"Bea, I know you are upset with me but I can explain."

"Explain what Dino? Explain that because I didn't sleep with you, you faded to black?" "Or maybe I'm not sophisticated enough for a millionaire like you? Or is it billionaire? I don't know what it is you want to explain to me but it does not matter. Now if you'll excuse me, I have to get home."

"Bea, I'm here because of Mr. Ross." I stopped dead in my tracks with my car door swung open.

"What about Mr. Ross?"

"He's dead Bea."

"Dead?? How? Who? I don't understand." Dino sat me down in the driver's seat and entered in on the passenger's side.

"He died of a heart attack, right there on the job. I didn't get in touch with you because when I first heard the news, I felt I needed the details before I made contact. So, I flew out here right away to investigate his death."

"Why you? Why would you fly out? You're just a client."

"No, I'm not just a client. I own the firm. I have for some time. Dave Ross and I go way back. He looked after me and took care of me when I was a snotty nosed kid drawing graffiti on city walls and sidewalks.

"Wait a minute…you said you had parents. Parents who were struggling immigrants that moved here to become entrepreneurs."

"I know. I lied. That is my fantasy childhood. The truth is I was abandoned by my Mother at the age of five, who was an immigrant from Panama. The place where I was born but never saw until I became wealthy. I was in the foster system until age 16. That's when I did time in Juvie for stealing a car. I finished my GED while there and made up my mind that I was going to be a drug dealer and never be broke again. Mr. Ross was leaving the office one night and saw me on the corner across the street from his office selling dope. He walked over to me and offered me a job. I couldn't imagine what he wanted me to do. He told me to stop by the office the next day and he would show me. You remember the life-like aquarium on his wall?" I nodded.

"I drew that and painted it, too. This man knew I had talent and he cultivated it. He saw to it that I enrolled and finished Art School in Cashew. He paid for every lesson. Then, when his wife became ill and soon died, he fell into a deep depression and almost lost the business due to overwhelming debt. He borrowed against the place to help with medical bills. At the age of 21, I was making one hundred thousand a year from billboard work alone. I took over the note to the office and eventually paid it off. I wanted to sign it back over to him but he wouldn't let me. So, you see Bea, he was like a father to me; the father I never knew or had. That's why I am here. That's why I wanted to be here with you. So, can you forgive me for not calling or showing up on Thursday?"

"You know what I thought though, right?"

"Yes, I know you thought I disappeared because you didn't spend the night with me. We've had enough conversations for me to understand what your Mother has instilled in you about men. But I assure you that Mama ain't always right, at least not this time." We held each other tight partly because of the loss of Mr. Ross and partly because we needed each other.

I whispered softly in his ear, "I forgive you."

So Much To Grieve

I had to face reality by going back home to Mama that night and I just didn't want too. I had no other choice. Dino insisted on coming with me in case Madelene became irate and he needed to rescue me. At this point, I felt like I didn't care if she became irate or not. I had just lost my boss and perhaps my job.

I turned the key in the door and yelled out that it was me and that I was home. When we walked in, the house smelled of gas. I walked toward the kitchen and there sat Mama. She had a cigarette in her hand getting ready to light it up.

"Mama! No! Stop!" I grabbed the cigarette out of her hand and looked at the burner on top of our gas stove. Dino stood in the doorway of the kitchen. Her plastic coffee cup had melted over the burner snuffing out the fire but the gas was still on. If she had lit that cigarette, she could have blown herself up.

"Mama, what are you doing?" I spoke in a calm voice.

"Oh, I was just heating up my coffee." She always drank instant coffee and what she thought she was doing was heating up the water for her coffee. What she did was place the instant coffee grounds in the cup and sat them on the burner, then turned the burner on to heat them up. I checked her pill box. She had only taken her meds once since I'd been gone the entire week. I don't think she noticed Dino was standing there. I called him a cab while he sat in the living room with both hands positioned around his head.

The death of Ross, coming in seeing my Mother like this, I think it all got to him that day. I apologized for her behavior but he would not hear of it. I

attended to her as Dino came in the kitchen and made sure the gas was off and that it was not leaking from a main line or anything. Soon the cab blew the horn and I sat Mama down in her gold high back chair and walked Dino outside.

"Thank you for coming with me, I really appreciate it."

"She's sick, Bea. You can't leave her. I've seen this before. I will be making funeral arrangements most of the week, so I will be around if you need to talk. Don't take that statement as a negative. You are important to me. I love you—I know I do. Things just have to straighten themselves out first before we can spend more time with each other."

"Of course, I understand. If there is anything I can do to help you with the arrangements, let me know."

"Thanks, I will." "I love you."

"I love you, too." The death of Mr. Ross did something to him unexplainable. I believe it was because Dino believed there was a God but he didn't really know Him.

Ross' death had affected me, too. I was going to have to look for another job. Moving out was put on hold once again. My never-ending story. No independence, no freedom, no future. When I wearied from feeling sorry for myself, I updated my resume' so that I could begin job hunting. Seawall was so small. I was blessed to have the job I had. I may not ever be that fortunate again unless I move. Move, it almost sounds like an obsolete word. I have tried and tried to live my own life, yet, I remain tied to Mama.

I attended Mr. Ross' funeral and when it was over Dino kissed me goodbye. He said he would get in touch with me the following week. He had to go back to Florida for business and would give me a call when he was back in Atlanta. He suggested that since I wasn't working full time, maybe I could come up for a couple of days. Yeah, and what excuse would I give Madelene for leaving this time when my boss was dead? I couldn't see that happening nor did I see any continued romance for Dino and me if I were stuck in Seawall. I drove up to the house after the funeral and saw all my clothes lying on the lawn. I was furious and had no idea as to why she was throwing my clothes outside.

"Mom, why are you throwing my clothes outside?"

"Because there is a man in the house peeing on all of them."

"A what?"

"I said that there is a man in the house peeing on all of your stuff and I can't stand the smell of that piss!" So now I am really upset trying to figure out how a man got by my Mother to get in the house, go to my room and pee on my clothes?? I grabbed the bat she kept behind the door to clobber this man in the head. I told her to show me where he was. She went to the door of my room and pointed toward my closet.

"See, there he is, right there. You see him?" There was no one there. Not a soul. I pretended I saw him, swung the bat a few times telling him to get out of my room and my Mama's house and pretended he left. Dino was right, Mama was sick. I gathered my things off the lawn as the neighbors on both sides watched and shook their heads. They knew she was sick, too. No one said anything, they just went back inside their houses. This made me cry so hard I could barely sleep. First, Mr. Ross; now something was wrong with Mama. I felt as if I would not see Dino anymore, either. I don't know, I fell into a deep dark place.

I Will Keep My Promise

Two weeks had passed and I was still bumming around trying to find full-time work—real work that would pay the bills for Mama. Seawall had little to offer except for labor, fast food or education. Okay, so maybe this was one of the times she was right, guess I should have become a teacher. (This is the one and only one time that I thought about teaching as a job for me.)

I made an appointment for Mama to see the doctor. I explained that Mama's medicine kept her from having frequent bouts of rage but now she would just sit and stare most of the time. She couldn't remember anything from one moment to the next. Once again, they ran test but this time the results were different. The results showed that she was in the first stage of Alzheimer's, a mental deterioration that can occur due to generalized degeneration of the brain. She was becoming senile. I discussed options and cures. Her doctor told me that so far there was not a cure but medication and monitoring would be the only secure way she would not harm herself or anybody else.

I thanked him and took her home. I begged God to show me what to do. She had always said that she didn't ever want to be placed in a nursing home because the people that worked there did mean things to people. I had promised her that I wouldn't do that. To keep my promise, I had to work part- time.

I found a job event planning. It was not going to be enough money to sustain us for a long period of time. You were paid by the events, which were few and far between in Seawall.

Control

When I walked in her bedroom and saw her sleeping, deeply, peacefully, I felt so sorry for her. I used to think I hated her but looking at her in this helpless state, I knew I did not. I couldn't. She was the only Mother I had ever known. Suddenly, the phone rang.

"Hello?"

"Bea, it's me. It's Dino."

"Dino, how are you?" Trying to sound cordial instead of excited.

"Listen, I'm going to be in Seawall tomorrow. Is there any way we can meet for lunch?"

"I'm not sure. Mom's been diagnosed with Alzheimer's and I have to line up someone from Social Services to stay with her when I am working, which I can only do part time. It's too late to request a caretaker now, so I don't know."

"No worries. I have stock in the Adult Daycare Center over on Bronze. We'll take her there while we have lunch. Will that be ok?"

"I suppose but she hasn't been around other people. She might freak out or something. I don't know, maybe."

"Listen, trust me. I know these people. I had a major part in screening them and hiring them. She will be fine. Besides, we will not be gone any longer than an hour so I can tell you the good news and we can eat. So, is it a go?"

"Alright, it's a go. I'll pick up you and your Mom around eleven thirty."

"That's fine."

"Good, I'll see you both then." This was going to be fun trying to convince her she was going to visit other people that she didn't know for an hour. I hope this works out. I started on her early the next morning while she was pleasant. For the most part, the meds kept her quiet and slow moving. I explained to her we were going for a ride and then for a visit. She didn't question a thing. When Dino arrived, I told her he was a good friend of mine and he was there during the gas stove incident. He would be giving us a ride to the visit. She said nothing.

Once we arrived, Dino introduced us to Katie, the Manager and she showed us around the place. It looked like a giant game room for old people. Some were playing dominos, others cards. Some ladies were doing dance exercises and others were knitting sweaters. It was really a cool place. Mama started to smile when she saw a lady light up a cigarette. Most of the time, she couldn't remember that she smoked. She started to walk toward her and I reached out to stop her. Katie grabbed my hand and told me to let her go. When she reached the lady, she automatically offered her a cigarette and they began to talk and laugh.

"You see, she'll be fine. Most of the patients here have Alzheimer's and get along well with each other. They may not remember each other the following day but in the moment they are fine."

I felt better so we left and went to have lunch at Pete's Diner about a mile away. The waiter took our order and Dino begin to talk. He apologized about not telling me the whole truth about his childhood and about being so distant from me after Mr. Ross' death. He explained that Alzheimer's was what Dave's wife died from and he recognized the signs in my Mother. He watched Dave lament and worry and exhaust himself with the changing stages of the disease and he didn't know if he could stick around and watch me go through it, too. He told me that at the time Dave was falling apart, the best he could do was bail him out of debt.

"But Bea, I am not going to leave you stranded, either."

"So, you're going to bail me out of debt, too?"

"No, because you are not anywhere near the debt Dave was in. You are just struggling trying to live off a lot less money than you used too. So, to make sure you regain the salary you once had and with the opportunity to make more, I am signing D&D Marketing Firm over to you."

"You're what?"

"You heard me. The firm is yours! You can keep it, sale it, hire, fire, rebuild, whatever you want. The property alone is worth over six hundred thousand dollars. I don't want you or your Mom to suffer for anything."

"Okay, so what's the catch?"

"There you go with that negative Mommy thinking again. Look here is the deed and here are the keys. I have already had the cleaning company to come in and clean and polish everything. Dave had a substantial budget and it looks like there is over one hundred thousand dollars in that account. Feel free to use that to replace furniture or décor as you see fit."

"Wow, this is amazing. I can't believe it. I just can't believe it!" And then it hit me, Mama.

"Dino, I can't go back to working full time. What about Mama? She can't be left alone by herself anymore. With me trying to get the firm back up to par, I would be paying out of the nose for someone to watch her 24/7."

"No, you will not. I have taken care of that, too."

"Oh really?"

"I have made arrangements for your Mom to reside in Cashew at the Mockingbird Quarters where she will be looked after and cared for as if she were their own relative."

"Mockingbird Quarters! That's the assisted living place where all the rich people live."

"Bea, there are some moderate-income people who reside there as well. It's just happens to be the best in this area."

"And how much is this going to cost me?"

"Mockingbird will take the monthly fees out of my business expense account for the next two years. D&D, with your management skills, will continue to gain profit. When the two years are up, I will switch the fees over to your expense account. If you keep the business, your business will pay for your Mother's care."

"Wow. I don't know what to say. Why are you doing all of this Dino?"

"I thought I told you already, I love you." He looked me straight in the eyes as he kneeled on one knee right there at Pete's Diner and proposed.

"Bea Faye, will you marry me?" The Tiffany Ring box exposed the second most beautiful two-carat Princess cut diamond I had ever seen.

Without hesitation, I screamed "YES!"

We embraced each other while the customers in Pete's all stood and applauded. We sat back down for a moment so that I could gather my thoughts. When I did, the first thought was about Madelene. Before I could speak, Dino had already saw my changed expression.

"Bea, I know you are concerned about your Mom and I don't intend to take you away from here for that reason. We will remain engaged for about a year until I can sell the business in Florida and the one in Atlanta. The one in Cashew will sustain itself."

"No, I can't let you do that. Those are your businesses that you worked so hard to build. I am not in favor of you selling them just for me."

"Sweetheart, it's not just for you, it's for us. Just stick with me and you will see. In a year's time, I will have a mansion built in this area. I've already started looking at land. It will be spacious for the kids."

"Kids?"

"You know because I was abandoned, I want to give my children the opportunity to have two good parents in a safe comfortable environment. The hour is almost up so we better get back to the Center and pick up your Mom." I planted a big kiss on his lips and told him thank you.

"The land I spoke about rests on at least twenty acres between Cashew and Seawall. It's just sitting there. It's listed on the market for Eighty Thousand dollars but in about six months, it will drop to half of that. Nobody is going to pay that kind of money to live in the country."

"You are so wonderful and I am so blessed."

"Lucky is what I call it. You are a lucky woman, Bea. Time to go."

I noticed that Dino rarely spoke in spiritual context. He would only mention God in comment or conversation. And since he traveled so much, I was certain that there was no church attendance. Truth is, I was so excited about someone showing me love and bringing Madelene along for the ride until I didn't dwell on it. If he believed, I could work with him.

When we walked in the Center, Maddy was laughing and talking with a couple of ladies and didn't notice we had arrived.

"Mom, we are here to take you home now."

"Home, so soon? I was just telling Lolly about my big sheep head fish I caught that time. You remember Bea? It was as tall as you were. Remember?"

"I sure do. I also remember being so afraid when you showed me it had real teeth."

"Real teeth?", Dino interrupted.

"Yes indeed, just like a human."

"That Bea is such a coward. She screamed and jumped all over the place and the damn fish was dead!" She and Lolly almost bust a gut laughing so hard. I just smiled.

"Hate to break this up ladies but I must be getting back to work, and Mom, Dino and I have wonderful news to share with you."

"Long as is it ain't about no nursing home, I'll listen. Those people over there kill old folks by making them sick and keeping them dirty. I'll break out if you put me there!"

"Come on, Mom."

I Must Choose To Live My Life

While riding in the car I thought about how I would try and explain that Mockingbird Quarters was NOT a nursing home but a five-star assisted living facility, the best in the area. It occurred to me that seeing would be believing. I would set it up with Dino to take her back to the Adult Day Care but on the way back home, we would take her to Mockingbird so she could see for herself. I helped her take off her sweater and sat her down in her high back gold chair so that Dino and I could share the news with her about the firm and the proposal. Then, we would talk about Mockingbird. She wanted to know who Dino was and why he was smelling around me.

"Dino and I have been dating for some time now. He was close to Mr. Ross, my boss that just passed away. I didn't say anything because I've been so concerned about your health. I pushed aside any personal activity to care for you.

"Hump, I see. So, if you pushed aside your personal activity as you say, why is he here now?" I began to tremble. It's the way she asked the question that brought on my fear.

"He's here, he's here now, uh."

"Mrs. Faye, I am here now because I have asked your daughter to marry me and she said yes."

"She said what? How could she say anything without asking me first?" Madelene looked at me with the scorching eyes of a demon as she spoke, "How many times have I told you about men and how they mean you no good. This boy right here has secrets, I can see it in his eyes. Once those secrets come to light, you will be sorry you every knew him."

"Mrs. Faye, honestly."

"Shut up! You are a fake and I know a fake when I see one. You are the type of man that convinces a woman that you are Mr. Right when you are Mr. Wrong. She is too stupid to know these things and because of that you are ready to take advantage of her. I say NO! Bea is not getting married to you or anybody else for that matter. What do you suppose she would do with me? Drop me off at some stinky, smelly nursing home somewhere—never to see me again? That will not happen! She will obey me and that's the way it has always been and that is the way it will always be. That's my little flat nose baby—not yours!"

"She is not a baby! She is a full-grown woman and it's time you realized that. Bea can make her own decisions!" With that Madelene raised up and took her Paul Bunyan left hand and slapped Dino so hard until he saw stars. Then she slapped me.

"How dare you let him talk to your Mother like that? Young man, it is time for you to leave." Dino looks at me and says, "Bea, if you are going to be my wife, you are going to have to leave your Mother and come with me." I knew I had to decide, I had to overcome the fear. Dino was right. It is my life and I must choose to live it.

"Mama, I will be back to pick up my things. I am going to be this man's wife regardless of what you think of him."

"Stupid ass! You'll see. He's going to break your heart, watch!" I went inside my bedroom and packed a suitcase while Dino booked the Penthouse at the Hyatt in Cashew for a week. I looked at my Mother and left. His hope was that things would die down between Madelene and me during the week and we would be able to get back on track. He would be in Florida all week finalizing business deals and back to Cashew by the weekend. Whether things were mended between Mom and I or not, he suggested I move to Atlanta.

"But what about the firm?"

"I know you are concerned but Bea, you don't really need to work. I could easily sell the firm to someone else and put you up in your own place in Atlanta until we are married. After experiencing your Mother's rage, I don't think it's safe for you to be around her."

"Dino, I've been around her all my life and I know how to handle it. I am not ready to move to Atlanta, yet. I want to work. I want to grow the firm.

And besides, you said that you looked at land to build a mansion for our family, right?"

"Yes, that is correct but I fear that your Mother will harm you if you stay here."

"I'll be fine, trust me. I will stay in the hotel for a week, then I will move back home with her until everything in Florida is done and our home is on its way to being built. Remember, this was the original plan to get the firm back on its feet and then get married and have a huge home for babies." Dino chuckled at the thought of being a father.

"You're right. Let's stick to the plan. I just don't want anything to happen to you. I love you."

"I love you, too and it won't."

What a week that turned out to be. I drove to Seawall every day to work and to check on Mama. The first couple of days she would not say a word to me. But I made sure she had food and the house was clean when I left. By the third day she said, "I am always right. You'll see you are making a big mistake. That boy's got a secret."

I would just say, "Yes, ma'am " and be on my way.

It was midnight Thursday of that same week when I received a call from the police department. They asked me if I knew Madelene Faye. I told them I did and that she was my Mother.

"We found her wandering the streets of the neighborhood. She was screaming and crying because she could not find her house. When we brought her back to the residence, the door was locked and she did not have a key. Apparently, she crawled out of her bathroom window because she thought she was in the wrong house. We had to force the door open but we've called a locksmith to repair it. How far are you away?"

"I'm about thirty minutes away but I am headed out right now."

"No problem. A female officer will remain here with your Mom until you arrive. Her name is Officer Torres."

"Thank you, officer."

"And ma'am?"

"Yes, sir?"

"You might want to look into getting your Mother some full-time help. She cannot be left alone."

"Thank you, I will."

Once I arrived, Officer Torres informed me that the locksmith had already been out and replaced the lock on the front door and handed me the key.

"Thank you so much for waiting until I arrived, Officer."

"No problem, she's such a sweet lady. If we can be of any other service, don't hesitate to call us."

"I won't and thanks, again."

Maybe Just Another Game

As Officer Torres left and I shut the door behind her, I saw Mom sitting and staring almost as if she wasn't aware of her surroundings. It's hard to believe that just five days ago she slapped the wits out of Dino and me and now she sits dazed and confused. Honestly, I wasn't sure if her dementia had advanced or if this was just a ploy to keep me from marrying Dino. Nevertheless, I was going to take her to the doctor tomorrow to find out.

"Mama, how are you feeling?"

"I'm fine. How are you?" Her sweetness indicated that she was abnormal in her thinking and not her true self. She allowed me to help her with her bath, take her medicine and put her to bed.

The officers had placed the screen back on the bathroom window and nailed it shut. That was one less thing I had to worry about. Thank God! It was almost three am and I was sleepy and exhausted. The plan was to go to the office extra early tomorrow to finish organizing and contacting clientel. With the need for a doctor's visit, I don't think work is going to happen at all tomorrow.

The next morning, I was up by eight, making an appointment for Mama which was scheduled for eleven and now it was almost nine thirty. I heard her stirring around as her feet shuffled toward the kitchen following the scent of coffee. I scrambled her an egg and made a piece of toast, her usual breakfast when she ate breakfast. She seemed alert and was ready to argue about the way I scrambled her eggs. Medication working. I informed her that she had a doctor's appointment at eleven.

"A doctor's appointment for what?"

"Mom, you had an episode last night. You climbed through the bathroom window looking for this house because you thought you were in another house."

"That's a damn lie! Does it look like I can crawl out of that small window, tall as I am? I don't know why you are trying to make me think that I'm crazy just so you can marry that liar but I'm not crazy!"

"Crazy has nothing to do with it. It has to do with your medication."

"That's why I don't like taking that mess."

"Understood. But when you don't take it, incidents like last night will continue to happen. It's dangerous. You could really harm yourself or somebody else. That's why I want you to see the doctor so he can explain what is going on with you."

"There ain't nothing going on with me except you scheming trying to get rid of me. I'm not going!"

"Mom, please, I'm worried. The police found you wandering around the neighborhood and called me. The proof that something is going on is the fact that you don't recall what happened at all."

"The police came?"

"Yes, ma'am. They had to break the lock on the door because you didn't have the key to get back into the house. Which makes sense if you didn't think it was your house. They repaired and replaced the lock and I have the new key."

"All this went on last night?"

"Yes, ma'am." Her entire demeanor changed.

"Why can't I remember? Why?"

"Mom, you have Alzheimer's, a slow deterioration of the brain. The doctor prescribed medication to try and keep the condition from advancing. When you don't take it, you hallucinate— see things, can't remember things and that's what happened last night."

"Maybe I should go and see the doctor so that he can tell me what's really going on with me."

"Maybe you should." Her face showed worry and dismay for the first time in a long time.

Once we were done with her primary care physician, we were sent to a neurologist for a brain scan. This process was lengthy so while waiting, I called Dino. Detailing what took place over the last twenty-four hours was like reliving a nightmare. I suggested that he cancel the Hyatt for the rest of the week because I knew my Mom needed me.

"I'm not concerned about cancelling a hotel room. I'm concerned about you and how you are holding up."

"I'm good and I know God will pull her through this."

"Okay, if you say so. But just know that I'm here for you. I'd originally planned to be there for you by the weekend."

"What happened?"

"The buyer for the Florida store was delayed by some unexpected business he had to take care of. We were scheduled to meet on Friday but now, it's rescheduled for Monday. I was going to fly in because I miss and love you, my future bride." I blushed a little.

"I love and miss you, too. Listen, the neurologist looks like he's headed this way with the results of the scan."

"Okay, go ahead and take care of your Mom. I'll call you later."

"Are you Bea, Ms. Faye's daughter?"

"I am."

We sat down in the waiting room while he went over the results. He shared the news that the dementia was now entering the second stage of Alzheimer's and that she would be drifting in and out of memory. Drifting in and out of memory, what did that mean? He further explained that in the early stages, she would struggle with short term memory. Things like what she ate for breakfast or even if she even she ate breakfast. She may even remember the day before that she has an appointment, but when the day arrives, she can't recall whether she does or not.

"My suggestion to you is to place her in a long-term facility that specializes in Alzheimer's patients. The disease is incurable and grows worse with time. It can also be taxing on family members trying to keep up with remembering everything for them. Are you married?"

"No. Engaged."

"Congratulations. My reason for asking is because married couples find it easier to keep the patient at home and share the responsibilities of caring for them. Depending on their disposition and personality, it can either break or bond a marriage. Nevertheless, you don't have to make that decision, yet. I am going to send her home with a new medication that will make her a little drowsy at first. Once her system gets used to it, the drowsiness will cease. If there are any out of the ordinary episodes, call me right away. Other than that, take care of her, she seems like a real sweet lady."

"Thank you so much, Doctor."

"You are welcome. I'd like for you to set an appointment for me to re-examine her in about a month. I'll see you both then."

"Yes, sir." The nurse was bringing her out and she was wearing a mean face.

"Let go of my arm. I'm not an invalid. I can walk." The nurse let go.

"Bea, get me the hell out of here. I laid in that thing and I know it was zapping all the sense I have left right out of me!" I laughed and told her she would be fine, although I wasn't sure of that.

Still So Much Drama

For some reason, she had a taste for pizza. She never eats pizza but I stopped and bought a medium with cheese and pepperoni to carry home. I felt like I was sinking into a black hole. This was all so much to deal with. Back at home, she undressed and put on her faded blue and pink house dress and sat at the table to eat. I placed a couple of slices of pizza on her plate and -sighed.

"What is it Bea? Why you sighing and going on? Let me guess. It's something that doctor said, ain't it?"

"Mama, you are in the early stages of Alzheimer's and your memory will begin to fail you.

You won't be able to remember little things at first and as time goes on, it will be greater things. The doctor recommended that you move to an Alzheimer's facility so that you can receive the care you need."

"You a damn lie! I know that the doctor didn't tell you that. You just want to get rid of me so that you can marry that sneaky Bino! You can't wait for him to carry you away from me and never look back. I don't care whether that doctor said I need help or not, I'm not going nowhere! And you are going to stay right here and take care of me. After all I've done for you, you ungrateful heifer! I saved your pitiful life and this is how you treat me?"

"I'm not treating you bad. I am trying to explain to you what the doctor said. Reading about the disease is frightening and I am worried that harm will come to you."

"Liar! You are worried that harm will come to you! And it will. You'll see! Now get out! Get out of my house and don't you come back. You understand me? Don't you come back!"

"But what about my things. The rest of my clothes, my books and all my business folders?"

"They will be on the front porch by morning if I don't decide to burn them first. I hope you're happy now that you'll be rid of the only person who ever loved you, who will ever love you. You are going to regret all of this. God will punish you."

"Regret what? All I did was try and explain what is going on with you. I am trying to help you." Then something took over me and I began to tell her how I felt how she had controlled me and kept me from receiving scholarships and opportunities all my life. How she planted worthlessness in my head and made me believe I was ugly and would never amount to anything. How she ran off Tyreer by shooting him. About how she lied to me about where babies came from. The educational opportunities she made me miss and most of all, how she lied to me about my real Mother. (Unknown to Mama, I found out the real truth about my biological Mom from my sister.)

On my Own

I went to my room and packed up what I could as I headed toward the front door. I looked at her and I began to cry deeply and loudly.

"Bye, Mama."

I called Dino on the way back to the hotel and hoped that he hadn't had time to cancel the rest of the week after all. I was a wreck. I had never spoken to her that way in my entire life. I felt so sorry that I had. I felt sorry for her. Dino called the Hyatt and paid for me to stay there in Cashew until I could move elsewhere. He still had plans to fly down mid-week and he insisted on finding an apartment for me since I was kicked out of Madelene's house. So many things were going on inside of my head. Had I done wrong by telling her what the doctor said? All my life when she became upset with someone else, I would experience her wrath.

Prayer soothed me somewhat that night; yet, tears soaked my pillow. I should be happy that I am really on my own now—no more control, guilt, or abusive factors to plague me. Free to go where I want, do what I want, marry who I want without interruption or fear. So why am I still crying?

The next day, I went to the office and buried myself in work. If I stopped focusing on projects or cliental for any length of time, I would hear her voice, "Get out of my house and don't come back! You understand me?"

Those words pierced me to the core of my soul. All this time, I thought it was our house. The house that she and Papa built for themselves and their little girl. The house where I spoke out loud for the first time. The house where she verbally and physically abused me. The house where she checked my underwear at random or hung up the telephone while I was talking to someone she didn't approve of. The house where Papa lay on the kitchen's back door in the yard until the ambulance came to pick him up. The house where she accused Dr. Willis and the Board of Directors at Watson of being dirty old men who were plotting to rape me. Yeah, I thought it was our house because what went on inside there affected my life. Every single bit. Inside that house was a controlled environment that felt like imprisonment instead of freedom. Imagine growing up not being allowed to ask questions or share your thoughts for fear of being slapped into next week. So many nights, I wanted to cuddle up in my Mother's arms and share my fears and my dreams. As a little girl, I wanted to ask her if God was always right or just her? And did He teach her how to always make me feel so bad? Yes, I had questions that I could never ask Madelene Faye because of fear.

One time in Sunday School when I was about twelve years old, I remember the teacher saying,' God did not give us the Spirit of fear, but of power and love and a sound mind.' How true I felt that statement was. How smart God must have been to keep the good stuff like love and power and sound minds to give away to people. The way I saw it, God didn't want to hand out anything bad, so he gave that ability to cause a spirit of fear to my Mama! She did God a big favor because to me, she handled it better than He ever would have.

It's funny how you think when you are a child. That is where it all begins, isn't it? It's in those formative years that a parent can bring a child up with love, kindness, inspiration, understanding, protection, the adoration for God and the freedom to love themselves as God loves them. Or they can control their thoughts and actions using fear.

Dino arrived on a Friday instead of mid-week. I was so weary from driving the round trip from Cashew to Seawall every day until it appeared as if I wasn't happy to see him.

"Why all the doom and gloom? I thought that seeing me would help cheer you up. Guess I was wrong, huh?"

"No, you aren't wrong, I'm just tired."

"No worries, I have a relaxing evening planned for us."

"Do you always plan everything without asking the other person if that's what they want to do?"

"Whoa! Where did that come from? All I am trying to do is make you happy, Bea. That's all."

"It all sounds a little controlling to me. I told you I was tired."

"That's fine. We'll stay in and order room service, if that's what you would like to do Madame." The way he said 'Madame' like an old English butler made me chuckle.

"That will be perfect, sir."

"Then it is settled." After taking a long hot shower, I put on my African inspired caftan and lay down on the queen-sized bed to the right of the bathroom. Dino was in the shower, so I turned on the television to watch the news.

Is He Really Into Me

Seawall was so small until local news was broadcast from Cashew. Seawall was going through a drought and so on and so forth. Flipping the channels, I found nothing interesting to watch. Dino appeared from the bathroom in silk pajamas and a terry cloth bathrobe with the initials DM on them. He settled into the other bed and began to read some documents that had to be finalized by Monday morning. Grant it, I was no longer a virgin and I lived a decent non-promiscuous life, but I was beginning to wonder what my "future husband" would be like in bed. Neither he nor I discussed sexuality at all, nor did we partake in it. Being deprived of a lot of things in my life including sex, I just wondered, especially since here I was so close to him in a room with a closed door and he didn't try to crawl into the same bed with me. Oh well, running more than one business had to be exhausting and he was so ready to get everything finished in Florida and Atlanta until he was working around the clock. I dozed off when I felt his warm lips on my forehead as he stood over me.

"Sleep tight my beautiful bride-to-be." I opened one eye, smiled, and turned over falling into a deep sleep.

Morning smelled fresh with coffee and Danish rolls brought up by room service and left on the counter in our suite. I arose stretching and looking around for Dino. He was not in the bathroom or the adjacent study. He must have gone downstairs for something. Taking a delicious sip of Brazilian roast coffee and a bite from a Danish roll, I decided to get dressed and go exploring, hoping to run into my future husband. Our suite was on the very top floor where you could see the entire city of Cashew. It was an awesome sight in the mornings. Before my expedition, I stood out looking over the city thanking God for another day, for this man, for my new life. The thought of it all made me feel excited and free. Suddenly, sadness entered in. I begin to think about Madelene at home alone, ill. Perhaps Dino wouldn't mind taking the thirty-minute drive to Seawall, I felt that I needed to check on her. I am sure he won't mind; he's always so sweet to me. Where was he anyway?

As I entered the room from the rooftop, I heard the key at the door. Dino enters wearing shorts, a tee shirt, and a pair of tennis shoes. The shorts seemed rather short to me for a guy but maybe that's the way rich guys wore shorts.

"There you are. I was just about to go on a Dino hunt."

"Why?"

"When I woke up and looked around and couldn't find you, I became concerned."

"There's no need for concern. I went for a run and I didn't think I needed your permission."

"I wasn't indicating that you needed my permission."

"This Dino hunt mentality sounded a bit too much like your Mother. I refuse to be controlled by anyone or anything. I am my own man and I don't need anybody trying to track me down."

"Now, look who's being testy."

"Look, I don't mean to be harsh or anything, I just can't stand the idea of anybody trying to hold me down."

"I wasn't trying to hold you down Dino, I was just missing you." He smiled his quirky little sideways smile and held his arms out to me. We embraced each other and sealed it with a kiss.

"I'm sorry, Bea. I know I'm a piece of work. It's just that since my life started off so bad, I want to make sure that it stays good."

"Why wouldn't it?"

"There is always the possibility of failure, which I try and eliminate at all cost. Buying, selling off and investing are high dollar moves. If I don't make the right decisions at the right time, I could lose everything. Then, I would lose you if I couldn't offer you a nice life. We both have had rough situations with parents, I think it's time that we put that behind us and live our best lives ever. That's all I'm trying to do for us."

"I know that you want what's best for the both of us. You try so hard to make me happy. But I just want you to know I am not marrying you for your money, for your business or any of those things, I am marrying you because of your heart."

"Just be patient with me, Bea. As you Bible Thumpers say, 'God is not through with me yet'."

"We are not called Bible Thumpers. We are called Christians, Christ Believers."

"Alright, well ok. I am going to hit the shower and order breakfast or would you rather go some place to eat?"

"I think I'd like to go out today. I think I'd like to go to Seawall to check on my Mom. Is that ok? Dino? Did you hear me?" All I heard was water running. We weren't married yet. I felt as if we just had our first disagreement and I just received my first no response. When he came out of the bathroom, he was dressed and ready to go.

"I want to go and see my Mom."

"Can we at least have breakfast first? I'm starved."

"Of course, it's just that when I asked you as you were going into the shower, you didn't answer me."

"I thought I did. No problem. We'll eat and then we'll drive to Seawall to see your Mother."

"Are you sure she wants to see you?"

"I don't know but I'm about to find out." I did think about the fact that she might not want to see me. I had prepared myself for the rejection just in case. On the other hand, maybe she missed me, maybe. Still, she was alone.

Chapter Twelve
ONWARD

The drive from Cashew to Seawall is about thirty minutes. I was quietly thinking about the tiff Dino and I just had and heard Madelene's voice in my head saying: *He's got a secret.* We barely spoke to each other on the ride over. I kept thinking did I really want to be married to a man who called me a Bible Thumper? We were at the half-way point when he said he had to stop and make a phone call. Pulling into a small café, he hops out of the car and goes inside. I was going to ask him to bring me a coke but he left too quickly. Why was this phone call so important? He had been gone almost twenty minutes when he returned to the car.

"Sorry about that Bea, business."

"Is everything going alright with your projects?"

"Yeah, everything is fine. A few glitches here and there but that's to be expected with something this big." The silence continued after that.

As we were approaching the outskirts of Seawall, we were held up by two fire trucks and an ambulance. It was rare that any tragedies happened in this small town so now my curiosity was peaked.

"I wonder what's going on?"

"It's looks as if they are headed into your neighborhood so we will soon find out."

My neighborhood! My heart started beating fast. Panic was about to set in. What if it was my house? What if it was Mama?! Dino seemed to suddenly drive slower. I was anxious to see where the fire was in my neighborhood.

She Was All Alone

Just before the entrance to my street the police had set up a barricade that kept us from moving forward. I jumped out of the car and explained to them that the fire could be coming from my Mother's house and she lived alone. They let us in and we slowly approached the middle of the street where my house sat. Fire was blazing from the roof of the house next door—Mrs. Cole's house. Mama was being brought out of our house on a stretcher. Dino gathered information while I tried to reach Mama and ask her what happened. Everyone was outside and the news stations were there along with two ambulances and two fire trucks. They brought Mrs. Cole's body out in a bag. She didn't make it. Mama was delirious and was rambling something I could not understand.

I motioned to Dino, who was talking to the fire chief, that I was riding in the ambulance to the hospital with Mama. He mouthed an okay. I began to ask how the fire started and from which house. They didn't seem to know those details just that my Mother was suffering from third degree burns on her legs and smoke inhalation. Mama was rushed to the emergency room while I registered her information. Shortly after, Dino shows up with what happened. It appears that Mrs. Coles' house had a gas leak, she lit a candle and sat it near her gas stove in the kitchen. The house exploded and the blaze engulfed Madelene's bedroom which is adjacent. That entire side of our house was destroyed.

Mama was taking a nap. I cried my eyes out waiting for information from the doctors as to what would be next for her. Finally, they informed me that she would be going into emergency surgery to try and save one of her legs, there was little hope for the other one. Dino couldn't seem to take the pressure of my sadness, so he left me there at the hospital. I was alright with that because I would not rest until she came out of surgery. I fell asleep in the surgery waiting room. I was awakened by the surgeon that was taking care of Mama.

"Are you her daughter?"

"Yes, I'm Bea."

"The way she spoke of you right before surgery, I thought you were a small child. Listen, I will get straight to the point. We had to amputate her left leg. It was burned too badly to try and graph. The right leg is damaged but she can survive with that one leg if." "If…"

"If what?"

"If she didn't have a cancerous tumor on her brain. Prior to surgery, she was speaking in a delirious manner which normally ceases after a powerful and affective pain injection. We use this injection on most burn patients, and it usually decreases their pain to silence. But she became hostile and very violent. Therefore, we wrapped her legs and called in a neurologist. He found a tumor on the frontal lobe of her brain and it is growing rapidly. He will come and speak to you in a few moments. She will be hospitalized for quite some time and that's if the tumor stays at a manageable size." With that he walked off. I sat there in a state of shock. I couldn't believe this was happening.

The neurologist came in and sat down to have a long talk with me. His news was worse than the surgeon's. He informed me that the growth of the tumor on her brain was growing so rapidly that in a week or two she would lose all use of her speech, sight, and movement of her arms. Because she was in her sixties, brain surgery would be too risky, especially with the amputation and the third-degree burns.

"I'm afraid that your Mother is not going to be with you much longer. We are going to do all we can to make her comfortable. I am so sorry."

"Thank you."

I was numb. Brain dead numb, movement numb, just numb. I stared into space for what seemed like an eternity. A nurse came into the waiting room to check on me and brought me a cup of coffee and a blanket. I sipped on the coffee, laid down on the leather love seat, covered myself and cried myself back to sleep. The next morning when I opened my eyes, Dino was sitting across from me.

"Good morning, Bea."

"Morning."

"I'm so sorry about your Mom."

"How did you know? You weren't here?"

"I came back about three in the morning and found you sleeping. I let them know that I was a part of your family and they told me everything. So once again, I'm sorry." He sat by me as he held me in his arms.

"What am I going to do?"

"Well, you are going to spend as much time with her as you can and, as you Christians believe, let His will be done." That statement made me feel uncertain about Dino for the second time. Why wasn't he a Christian after all he's been through? Did he think his rough life was God's fault? I don't know anything anymore. I had to pray.

I left Dino in the waiting room while I found the hospital Chapel. I talked to God long and hard about Mama and that's when I heard Him say: Forgive her. I needed to see her to tell her I forgive her. Since she was in ICU, I had to wait for the next visitation hour. That left enough time for me to go back to Cashew to the hotel to shower, change and drive back down.

Maybe Mama Was Right, Sometimes

After Dino dropped me off at the hotel, I felt certain that I would have the chance to talk to Mama again. I knew that God had heard my prayers. I was looking for my hairbrush in one of the bathroom vanity drawers when I ran across something that shook me to the core: condoms. It might not have bothered me as much if they were stored there for future wishful thinking. But there was a pack of two, with one missing. As if I didn't have enough to deal with, now the assumption that Dino was cheating on me soared anxiety to a new level. I could barely move toward the shower. Once inside, I drifted away in my mind to the days of Tyreer. I knew in my heart that was my pre-approved by God soul mate that she ran away. Now, my anxiousness to be loved by someone had overpowered my logic. Obviously, this man didn't love me. Now, it looks as if I have two people to forgive—Dino and my Mama.

After cleaning up, I was ready to go back up to the hospital. Going back into the bathroom to take another look at that used package of condoms, I needed a way to approach this. Suddenly, I became consumed with who, where and when? I knew that he and I had never had any sexual contact— ever—so who was she and when was he with her? The phone rang which startled me. Trying to calm my breathing down, I picked up.

"Hello?"

"Who is this?" A male voice inquired.

"Uh, excuse me sir, but who is this?"

"Where is Big Daddy D?"

"Who? Sir, I think you might have the wrong number. There is no one here by that name."

"Is this the Hyatt Penthouse Suite 1020?"

"How would you know that?"

"Either you are as dumb as a doorknob or as blind as a bat. This is D's hangout for his, let's just say…special guest."

"Oh really?"

"Yes, girl really. I thought sure you knew. He doesn't deal with many women unless he thinks he has found someone who can have babies. Someone who he thinks can measure up to that forthcoming Maze inheritance."

"Listen, I have to get back to Seawall. I have a sick mother in ICU but I would love to continue this conversation. Is there any way I can meet you later over coffee?"

"Listen, the only reason I am telling you any of this is because he owes me money for my services. I used to be one of his most popular escorts until I decided to get out of that end of the game. But I have provided him with some of the best top gay male escorts in the business and I receive a percentage of what they make. He stiffed me on my take and I am mad as hell! Sorry you had to witness his "coming out", so to speak, in this manner, Princess. But I need my money!"

"Listen, if I find a way to get you your money, would you tell me everything and I do mean everything?"

"I suppose I could arrange that."

"Good, then meet me downstairs in the Breakfast Club tomorrow morning at eight. My name is Bea."

"Yeah, I know Bea Faye, his new wonder woman."

"Since you already know my name, I think it's only fair that I know to whom I am speaking."

"Fair enough, Lucas."

"Alright Lucas, I'll meet you in the Breakfast Club tomorrow morning at eight."

"Done!"

When we hung up the phone, I was heart hurt—a mother that had been predicted not to make it and a fiancé that was running a male escort service and obviously testing out the merchandise. I could hear those haunting words coming from Madelene's lips: *"That boys got a secret."* I prayed and talked to myself all the way back to the hospital. I could not let on that I knew as much as I did to anyone.

All of this explains why we were never sexually intimate with each other, why he never attempted to make that happen. I can't believe this. I couldn't wait until I spoke with Lucas, especially the bits and pieces about inheritance and babies. This man was using me to gain wealth. *'Lord, help me please!'*

Back in ICU, the nurse told me that Mama's organs were attempting to shut down one by one, especially her lungs. She could not leave this Earth until I told her that I forgave her for all the misery she caused me in my life. She just couldn't die yet.

"Can I see her?"

"Not yet. We are giving her breathing treatments right now. Perhaps in an hour or so. Feel free to go down to the cafeteria or the lounge until she is ready to be seen. She doesn't have strong breath or speech left, so when you do go in, speak briefly. It's best for her not to feel pressured to speak at all. But if she chooses to talk, let her talk and then you speak. That way she would have had the opportunity to speak to you because there will be so little breath left."

"I understand. I will return in about an hour."

"See you then. Oh and Ms. Faye…"

"Yes?"

"I'm sorry." The tone of a condolence sounded so earth shattering.

On my way to the elevator, I saw Dino coming in my direction. I found it hard to look at him. He gave me a hug and asked how

Mama was doing. I gave him the update and I told him I was on the way to the cafeteria and if he would care to join me. He said he would sit with me for a while but he needed to pack a bag to head to Atlanta in the morning. The sale of the Atlanta factory would be finalized then.

"You seem so quiet Bea— removed. Listen, I know

accepting death can be a hard pill to swallow but we all must come that same way someday." Inside my head I was thinking, yeah, some sooner than others depending on their lifestyles. I remained silent.

Then, I thought about Lucas and the money. I never asked how much Dino owed him. I had to come up with a plan to have some available cash on me by tomorrow morning. I reached out and touched his hand, quivering inside at the thought that I didn't know where his hands had been. I told him that my Mom's mortgage was due on the house and that she paid with a money order all the time. I would need direct cash to pay it for her because she didn't write checks either.

"How much do you need?" Lord, I had no idea.

"At least five thousand dollars."

"Wow! She pays that kind of mortgage in that old neighborhood?"

"Not all at once. The plan is to pay it up for at least three months because I don't know what is going to happen. She may need to go back there and instead of using her social security benefits on mortgage payments, she can use it to improve her daily living. Just like she did when I lived with her."

"That sounds like you are expecting her to live."

"It's not over until God says it's over."

"If you ask me, according to all the reports from the doctors, it is over."

"How dare you say that? You are not God!"

"Contrary to rumor, some people think I am." I was about to lose focus. I had to refocus on getting the money. Calm down Bea.

"Regardless of what other people call you, (Big Daddy D.), can you help me out? I know it sounds like a lot but to be honest with you, I need to pay her mortgage and allow myself a shopping spree or something. I am so stressed over all that has happened."

"Hey, sweetheart, the money is no problem. I will leave you one of my cards."

"Wait, remember I told you she does everything cash."

"Oh yeah, that's right. Old people. They have such a hard time with change and readjusting to it. So, while you are in visiting with your Mother, I will run to my bank and get the cash for you. Is that alright, Princess?" Princess? That's the first time he called me that and the second time I heard it today.

"That will be fine and I appreciate you so much."

"Anything for the future Mrs. Maze." I looked at my watch and realized that the hour was almost up. We hugged and parted ways.

Back in the ICU, the nurse informed me that Mom was not doing so well. Her breathing had become much shorter than it was before I went downstairs. I still had to tell her what was on my heart but she has had a rough day.

"Would you mind coming back in the morning?" We can only hope that things will be better with her by then."

"Yeah, sure. I will be back first thing tomorrow morning."

While walking out, I remembered that I had a meeting with Lucas the first thing tomorrow morning. I didn't know how to reach him to reschedule the time. It was important that I talked to Mom and it was important that I talk to Lucas, too. I didn't know how that would be possible. Mom was here in Seawall and the hotel, where I was to meet Lucas, was in Cashew. Think Bea, think.

I had to hang around until Dino came back with the money. Therefore, I waited in the front lobby so that I could see him when he walked in. In the meantime, I wondered if the hotel's front desk would have a record of all incoming calls to the suite. If so, that would give me access to the number Lucas called from. If I reached him, the meeting could be rescheduled for around eleven instead of eight. I wasn't sure if it would work but I had to try. Walking over to the hospital's information desk, I asked to use the phone.

My hunch was right. The hotel faxed over to the hospital the call record for our suite. After being directed to the Business Center, I picked it up the fax and noticed an unfamiliar number. That call had to be from Lucas according to date and time. Less than thirty minutes after that call, another call came in. I had left the room by that time. *Curiosity killed the cat*…Madelene used to always say and I was a curious cat for sure. Nonetheless, I returned to the lobby and just in time. Dino was walking through the revolving glass door of the hospital. Quickly placing the phone record in my handbag, I sat faceless and motionless.

"What happened? Didn't the visit go well?"

"They wouldn't let me see her. They suggested that I come back in the morning."

"Wow, I'm sorry. Perhaps we can leave here and go pay her mortgage and while we're out get some shopping therapy underway. What you think?"

"I think I just want to go back to the hotel and rest. All of this has been so hard on me. I will take care of the mortgage in the morning but for now, let's just go."

"Are you sure? I mean I could go pay it for you and that would be one less thing for you to stress over come tomorrow."

"I said I will do it in the morning. There you go, always trying to be in control. I want to go and pay it when I want to, not when you want to. Let's just go."

We spoke not another word to each other. In the scheme of things, this was perfect. He could not stand defeat so I knew once back at the suite, he would leave again. It was less than a half hour when he slammed the five thousand dollars on the table and took off out the door. I was so glad because I really needed to get in touch with Lucas. The phone rang several times. When he finally answered, I told him the situation and that I needed to meet him at eleven instead of eight.

"That might be a problem, Princess. I have business in Seawall tomorrow and won't be returning to Cashew until the following day. I had planned on leaving after we met at eight."

"Perfect!"

"Perfect? How So?"

"My Mother is in the hospital in Seawall and I am headed there in the morning. Why don't you meet me at St. Anthony's Hospital in the Cafeteria at eight instead? That way I can visit with my Mom and give you the money all at the same time."

"I suppose that could work. But since our last conversation, it occurred to me that I never gave you the amount of money he owes me."

"I know. So, what does he owe you?"

"He owes me four thousand dollars because he only gave me ten thousand of a fourteen thousand deal." I thought to myself, what do these escorts do for that kind of money?

"No problem, I have it and I will give it to you in the morning."

"Great. Good job, Princess. I can't wait to meet you and bring you up to date on Mr. Maze, Honey."

"I'm looking forward to it. See you in the morning." When I hung up the phone, I sat staring at the other number on the call report. I dialed it.

"Amazing Escort Service, specializing in bondage and submission. How may I direct your call?" I hung the phone up.

How could this be happening to me? I wasn't perfect but I wasn't a bad person either. Being raised under the iron fist of Madelene made me too afraid to be bad. I knew who God was. I worshipped Him, read His Word and depended on Him to keep me alive. So why was my life so bound? What were the chains that kept binding me? *'I want to be free, Lord! Please set me free!'*

Who Is This Man

When I arrived at the hospital, Lucas was in the cafeteria waiting for me. Boy! Did I get an earful that day! It turned out that Dino had escort services across the United States And included locations in Atlanta, California, Colorado, DC and Florida. Lucas explained to me that Dino used to be an escort himself. It was the way he made money to survive. The t-shirt design companies are real but also serve as a cover for the escort services. He told me he was an investor in the services along with several other major players across the States. The part about the inheritance was all about his mother who was an immigrant who married a big-time gangster in New York. She hired a lawyer to track Dino down without him knowing she existed or her lifestyle. Before she died, she set up a huge inheritance of over two million dollars for Dino. A specification for him to be awarded the money is that he had to be married and have at least one child. If he managed to have two children, the inheritance would gain another one hundred thousand dollars.

"So, this is where I come in?"

"I'm afraid so, Honey. I am not going to say he doesn't love you or anything but he has a lot at stake, especially being gay to the core. Another requirement is that he had to get out of the business. Which is probably why he is looking at land in Seawall, somewhere nice and quiet and undetected. You know my Mama taught me that bad karma follows you wherever you go. I just hope you don't let it follow you. Thanks for the chat and the cash. I've got to run."

After the meeting with Lucas, I was discouraged and angry. I knew I should go upstairs and try to talk to her but I wasn't in the right spirit. I called the nurses' station instead to inquire about her condition. The response was the same. She was hanging in there although her organs were shutting down. Her speech was slow and slurred. Not a lot of change from yesterday. I assured them that I would come back that evening because I needed to talk to her. The nurse said she would look forward to my visit and we ended the conversation.

I was so consumed with the previous conversation with Lucas until I couldn't think straight. I decided that I would drive back to the hotel, pick up my things and reserve a room here in Seawall near the hospital. I wasn't sure how I was going to approach Dino with the fact that he was using me to gain an inheritance. What a low life! Back at the hotel, I was almost done packing when Dino steps in the room.

"Bea, where are you going?"

"I'm going to check into a hotel near the hospital. Mama is dying and I need to talk to her before she leaves this world."

"What could you possibly tell her at this late date? And what if she doesn't understand?"

"All I know is that I have to try."

"Let me help you. I'll set you up in a nice hotel. It's not close to the hospital but I can have a driver take you wherever you need to go."

"No, thanks. I choose to drive my own car, book my own hotel room without your assistance."

"Bea, what is the matter? Did I do something wrong? Talk to me."

"Not now, Dino. I have to go and prepare to see my Mother."

"Your Mother! Oh wow, this is a switch. After all the emotional, verbal, and physical abuse she laid on you, you care? What a dumb ass! I made sure that I would not be abandoned or abused by anyone every again in my life. There is no way I would forgive them for what they've done."

"I know you wouldn't. You don't know God. I don't think you know He exist. Therefore, I understand that you don't understand and that's okay. Because understanding comes with time. The more time passes, the more I understand things."

"What's that supposed to mean?"

"Like I said, we will talk later." He grabbed my arm and I slapped him.

"Don't you every put your gay, bisexual or whatever you are hands on me again.!" I left him standing there in a daze. I didn't intend to say that but he grabbed me. The defensive monster in me, inherited from Madelene, came out.

Driving back to Seawall, it all came down on me. I started to sob uncontrollably. So much so until I had to pull to the side of the road. If I only had Papa. He had moved to Browns Gate which was about two hundred miles away. I didn't have his phone number or address. Madelene forbade him to come anywhere near me or her or else she would shoot him. My life right now is a mess. Madelene is dying; Dino is gay; and Tyreer, the man I really love, doesn't want to have anything to do with me. At least, I am determined to fulfill my mission. I am going to tell Mama that I forgive her for all the restrictions she placed on my life; for all the fear and heartache she caused me. I know if I get that off my chest, my life will get better.

The Truth Always Come Out

I checked into the Holiday Inn about two blocks from the hospital. I had lunch and started to read the local newspaper. The paper was a news combination of both Cashew and Seawall. The news for both towns put together may have been five pages. On Page Two was a picture of Lucas! The headline read: *Male Prostitution Ring Mogul Agrees To Speak Out.* I read the article in disbelief. I had just sat with this man a few hours earlier. Turns out that the FBI had been watching this operation for quite some time. They were interested in who set it up and why was most of the money untraceable. Lucas had agreed to tell all. Oh no, I thought I solved that problem by giving him the money. Now, he was going snitch on him! The authorities took Lucas to jail until he could post bail. I had to get down there to convince him not to do this to Dino. I thought they were close friends. I headed down to County Jail and asked to speak with Lucas. They told me that he could not speak with anyone because he was under interrogation. Although, I had planned on ending it with Dino, I didn't want it to end with him behind bars. Leaving out, Dino was coming in. He was in total shock as to why I was there.

"Bea, what are you doing here?"

"I came to see Lucas."

"What? Lucas?"

"I know you came to bail him out, Dino. I know everything. I answered a phone call in the suite, Lucas was on the other end. He told me you cheated him out of some money. I agreed to meet with him and pay him what you owed. At that meeting he told me who your really are and why you really want me as your wife. It's all about the inheritance isn't it? Answer me! Isn't it!?"

"Bea, I..ne…"

"Shut up! I came down to try and convince Lucas not to expose you but looking at you now, trying to deny who you are, I don't care what happens to you."

"And I don't care what happens to you either. Country and homely chicks like you are a dime a dozen. I can always find someone else to fill your shoes."

"That's if you're not locked up!"

"Trust me little girl, I am too powerful to ever get locked up. You'd be surprised how many important businessmen I have in my back pocket who patronize my services. All I would have to do is make a phone call and their worlds would fall apart. So, don't go getting happy about my demise, there isn't one." He walked off with confidence and I walked out with lack of it. I waited around for him to come out because I wanted to tell him that I forgave him; that I had to get to Heaven by any means necessary because this old earth had been pure Hell. I never had that chance.

My Last Chance

It was early evening, so I headed back to the hospital. They finally let me in to see her. She looked so frail, small and uncertain. She had aged considerably. The lower part of her leg was missing, wrapped in gauze and the other wrapped in a compression wrap.

"Mama? How are you feeling?" She slowly turned her head over to look at me. Her lips were parched and scaley. Inside the drawer beside her bed was a tube of Vaseline petroleum jelly. I took my index finger and smoothed it over her lips. She spoke in a whisper.

"Thank you, Miss Lady." A huge tear ran down my face.

"I haven't seen you before. What is your name?" I sat down beside her bed and took her hand in mine.

"My name is Bea."

"Bea? That was my daughter's name. She was my pretty little flat nose baby. Sometimes, I don't think I told her that enough. I know I should have told her why I was so hard on her."

"You never told her?"

"Naw, I thought if I told her, she would hate me." The nurse interrupted us with vitals. Once she left, I picked back up the conversation.

"Why did you think Bea would hate you?"

"Are you a doctor, one of them doctors that take care of people that are sick in the head?"

"Oh no, ma'am. I'm, I'm a friend of Bea's"

"Bea? Who is that?"

"You said she is your daughter."

"Was my daughter."

"Did something happen to her?"

"I think so. I remember a fire and I could hear her crying. I tried to run over to get her out of the fire, but I couldn't. Next thing you know, I ended up here." The nurse reentered.

"You must leave now. She has talked enough for today. Feel free to come back tomorrow." I looked at my Mama before I headed toward the door when she said, "See you again sometime, Miss Lady."

Stopping by the nurses' station to get an update on her condition, the news was not good. The tumor was enlarged which sped her into the third stage of Alzheimer's. She didn't know who I was. I wanted her to know who I was, so she'd know that I had forgiven her.

"Would it be alright if I stopped by tomorrow?"

"Of course." I did a lot of praying on my way home that night. Asking God to give me the opportunity to let her know how I felt. If He could just let her be in her right mind tomorrow morning, I would be so happy.

This Is It

It was three o'clock in the morning when something told me to get up and go to the hospital. As I approached the ICU, I saw the doctor and two nurses coming out of Mama's room with grim looks on their faces. I started to cry because I thought she was gone.

"You better hurry, I think this is it." I walked inside that room and her caramel-colored skin had turned dark and ashy.

"I forgive you, Mama. I really do." She couldn't speak but she motioned for me to look in the bottom drawer of the bedside dresser. In the bottom drawer was a rumbled up brown paper bag. Inside was a dirty and dusty envelope.

"Tell me what you want to do with this?" Her eyes were slowly closing.

"MAMA! Tell me what you want me to do with this! Tell me, Mama! Tell me please!" There were no words as she flatlined into Glory. It was over. The only Mother I had known was gone. I watched in silence as the coroner documented her cause of death. Shortly after, the local undertaker came to pick up her body.

When I reached the parking lot of the hotel, I realized I hadn't let go of the dingy brown paper bag. Once inside, I opened it up and pulled out the old envelope that was brown and yellow with time. Inside was a letter. The words on the paper were almost faded. I sat wondering how long she had kept this letter and who was the letter to? Why hadn't she mailed it or given it to the intended receiver? Mama couldn't read or write well so I knew I was going to have to decipher what was written on that faded paper that night. It took hours that night trying to understand what she had written on the front and back of that old piece of paper. This was the translation:

Bea,

I'm gone try and tell you some things. Maybe then, you will understand why I was the way I was with you. Your Mama was my niece, the daughter of my half-sister that my Daddy made. She lived back off in the woods near the people I worked for. My boss, his name was Mr. Gray. He had a ranch hand named Big Joe. Mr. Gray and Big Joe took turns doing bad things to me at night.

One day in the cool of the evening, your Mama, Fannie, come skipping down in them woods near Gray's ranch. She was happy cause berries was out and she could pick some to feed her other children. I saw from the window Big Joe sneaking up on her. He put his hand over her mouth and laid her down on the ground. I was angry because I couldn't do nothing about it. Big Joe is your Daddy and I feels guilty cause I worked for them people. So, I made her give me you. I knew she could never protect you from the evil men of this world but I could and I would. I promised her that what happened to her, and to me, would never happen to you. I know you feel like I didn't love you but I did. I ain't good at showing it because I never learned how.

I had to fight my way through everything to make it in this world. I didn't want you to have to do the same thing. So, I'm to forgive me if I have messed up your life in anyway. Please forgive me.

Mama,

The pages were old and the ink almost faded but I held on to that letter for dear life. All that she put me through was to keep me from going through. I don't suppose she knew how to do it in a kind and loving way because she had no examples. What a rough life that must have been, having to work for someone at such a young age; having to do whatever task they put before you just to survive. I folded the letter up, placed it back in the envelope and put it back in the brown bag. I fell asleep with the bag still in my hand.

Mama passed on a Monday and although it was Wednesday, it had already been a busy week. The services were scheduled for Saturday morning at ten o'clock. On Saturday, a few people from the church showed up but that's about it. She was not a friendly person; therefore, she didn't have many friends. Family that was still alive came down to pay their respects and then just like that it was over.

The journey to forgiveness was over. It amazes me that after all these years, I knew I really needed to forgive her but she needed me to forgive her, too—forgive her for looking out for me and loving me the best way she knew how. The revelation is that I also needed to forgive myself for holding everything she did to me against her. No, Mama ain't always right but neither is unforgiveness. For if ye forgive men their trespasses, your heavenly Father will also forgive you: but if ye forgive not men their trespasses, neither will your Father forgive your trespasses Matthew 6:14-15.

It's right to forgive. I forgive you, Mama. I forgive you, Mama. It has taken me years to understand why I previously said those words but held unforgiveness in my heart. It felt so bad not to feel love from my Mother. It felt bad not to be trusted, to be called ugly or stupid. It really hurt to hear bad things about my biological mother, sisters, and brothers and to have them kept from me. Although there were times that physical abuse took place, it didn't outweigh the emotional abuse. It was the emotional abuse—the words—that damaged me from a child to a young adult. The words are what pierced me and made me feel so worthless. Proverbs 18:21 says, Death and life are in the power of the tongue: And they that love it shall eat the fruit thereof.

Her words killed me emotionally but spiritually, I did not die! It was the Spirit of the Lord that held me together. I'm not saying that my upbringing didn't have something to do with me trying to live righteousness but I know for a fact that the relationship I developed with the Savior is what has held me together. It's what has blessed me with a saved husband and a wonderful son. God can do what no other power can do.

I wanted to hang on to that unforgiveness so that I would not hold myself accountable for all the other mistakes I made in my life. I wanted to always blame her. It was so much easier to blame her instead of me. I needed to forgive, truly forgive. Once I absorbed the fact that if I didn't forgive, Christ would not forgive me, my heart changed. When I told her, I forgave her before she died, I meant that. But it has taken me eighteen years to feel it, deep down inside, feel it.

I had to share this story so that those who read it can feel forgiveness, too. Do not harbor it in your heart until the end of time. God's Word is not void. He will not forgive you unless you forgive others. Is unforgiveness worth eternal pain? No, it's not.

No, Mama ain't always right but neither is unforgiveness.

www.ingramcontent.com/pod-product-compliance
Lightning Source LLC
Chambersburg PA
CBHW031136160426
43193CB00008B/155